Social Media Marketing & Personal Branding

Explode Your Online Business And Brand, Influencing Your Audience Through Facebook, Instagram, YouTube & Twitter (Advertising, Blogging, SEO)

Joshua Reach

Social Media Marketing

Build a Global Online Business in 2019, Following The Marketing and Advertising Network Secrets Strategy Guide Through Instagram Facebook YouTube Twitter Pinterest and LinkedIn

Joshua Reach

Table Of Contents

Introduction

The importance of going worldwide

If you are a small business owner that wants to remain competitive, you should consider opportunities for wider reach and production efficiency by doing business at the international level. Some niches are super-competitive in some regions but have tremendous growth opportunities in others. When you take your business global, you will have access to the marketplace with nearly 7 billion possible customers. This is a huge opportunity that you should not ignore.

One of the primary motives of going global is definitely to find new income streams. Sometimes there is too much competition at the local scene while other times businesses will saturate local markets. Growth opportunities may dry up, and this may trigger the need to grow a business beyond local borders. When a business successfully navigates its way into multiple national markets, it gains access to a broader customer base and generates new business. This leads to increased profits while minimizing costs.

Benefits of going global

1. Acquire more customers: While the US has about 4 percent of the global population, other nations much larger populations. For instance, China is at 19 percent while India has 17 percent of the world's population. Such large populations present opportunities for businesses to acquire more customers.

2. Increase revenue streams: By accessing new markets and acquiring new business opportunities and customers, a business will definitely increase its profits by creating new revenue streams.

3. Numerous other benefits: There are numerous other benefits available for you. These include market development, access to a larger talent pool, gain better margins, reducing dependence on the local market, and increased supplies and resources.

New 2019 Strategies that will Blow your Mind

Innovation in marketing in this era is essential. As a business owner, you need to keep yourself updated with some of the latest trends in marketing and advertising. There are quite a number of innovations that will be adapted in 2019 that will help to take your business to the next level.

Multichannel and Omni-channel marketing

The term Omni-channel originated around customers in order to describe marketing strategies that exist outside the travel and retail sectors. Omni simply means every kind, all, or the whole. Therefore, Omni-channel marketing refers to reaching out to customers and interacting with them across all possible communication channels. Even then, a focus should be placed on budgets so that only the most effective channels are selected.

As a business owner, getting online is no longer sufficient. You need to create a mobile responsive website. Such a website should also focus on speed and personalization. They should have a conversational user interface in order to create the ultimate customer experience.

Virtual and augmented reality: Businesses are now using mobile cameras in order to improve customer experience. Through both virtual reality and augmented reality, you can promote brand engagement and also make the pre-purchase decision much easier for your customers. The process will almost bring your products to life. Your customers will be able to make life much easier and better for your customers.

Artificial intelligence: Not many business owners or digital marketers make use of artificial intelligence. Yet it is a powerful tool that can be incorporated into your overall marketing strategy.

Artificial intelligence is useful when it comes to improving user experience and simplifying data-based experiences.

These are just some of the emerging and existing techniques that are expected to become really big in 2019. If you are not applying them as part of your marketing strategy, then you may lose out.

Reasons why you must master marketing and advertising

Every small business starts by, among other things, focusing on getting their first customers. Online businesses often target online shoppers, especially those connected via Smartphones and other devices. Others rely on traditional forms of advertising like coupon mailers and print ads.

However, while these strategies of hoping customers will find business may work, it is advisable to adapt marketing strategies that will prove successful in the long run. For instance, digital marketing enables businesses of all sizes to reach huge online audiences in a measurable and cost-effective manner.

However, there are other benefits to learning digital marketing skills. There are numerous others as well. These include getting to interact with prospective clients and finding out exactly what they are searching for.

Digital marketing methods are much cheaper compared to traditional marketing means which enables you to reach a much larger audience at very low costs. You also get to track responses to your marketing efforts which in essence enables you to find out what is working and what you can improve on.

Marketing is a worthwhile activity

Marketing is viewed largely as an expense even though in essence it is an investment. It is a crucial activity especially when it comes to attracting the attention of new customers and prospective clients.

You are able to develop services, and products demand and eventually turn prospective customers into actual customers.

Increased following easily translates into increased sales

As a business owner, you need to focus on increasing your presence on popular social media. This should be part of your larger digital marketing strategy. Most of your customers and prospective customers are on different social media. If you are not reaching out to them, then you are probably missing out on a huge opportunity.

The first thing you need to do is to expand your social media marketing channels. This means having a presence in as many media platforms as possible. The more popular ones include Twitter, Facebook, Instagram, YouTube, Pinterest, and LinkedIn among many others.

Since most of your customers are probably already on social media, you will easily be able to reach out them and encourage them to remain faithful to your brand. In the process, they will reach out to their followers and friends and introduce them to your brands.

If you have a multitude of followers, then they will reach out to even more friends and followers who will, in turn, introduce your products and brand. This way, you will be able to attract even more customers. Therefore, open accounts and business pages on as many social media platforms as possible in order to attract more customers and enjoy increased sales.

The technology used is organic in nature so no need to spend a lot of money

Organic technology serves a huge purpose within the broader marketing context; the requirements are quite high. For instance, you will need to make use of ranking hashtags and also create your own hashtags when you post your own content. Hashtags keep your content relevant and expose your brand to a much wider global audience.

You need to put high-quality content out there for others to see. It could be a website full of well written, relevant content that appeals to customers around the world. Take for instance the social media website Instagram. This specific social media is perfectly designed for lifestyle photos and images.

Organic technology provides traders with a huge opportunity to promote their brands and build their businesses. Getting the chance to communicate your brand's values and lifestyles is one of the benefits of digital marketing. All the social media platforms offer different solutions and opportunities to business owners. Therefore, as a business owner, you should not be surprised when you see consumers dance to music from your establishment.

Some of the other effects of organic social media include the fact that possibly only 3% to 4% of social media followers viewing a brand's products costs. Other benefits you can expect include communicating brand values, validating your brand, attracting new, very cool wait outside. There are also other benefits including influencer relationships, and so much more.

Organic serves a useful purpose when it comes to the broader marketing strategy. Before you embark into the river, you should take a look at your cash flow statements, bank, and so on. This way, you will be able to determine your budget and how much you can afford to spend. You should also consider paid adverts at this stage. This is because social media services such as Facebook have minimized the effects or benefits of organic search. Such platforms favor paid searches so you may need to combine the two. What is undisputed is the fact that paid advertising is a lot more effective when compared to natural, inorganic, advertising.

For traders, or business owners, or digital marketers, there is no better place to nurture influencer relationships that on social media. Anyone on the PR team or influencer marketers, you will largely rely on social media to connect with others.

You Should Give, Give, and Give First and then Start to TAKE

If you want to be successful on social media and the internet, then you need to attract a huge following and then build trust. This process is very effective if you know how to handle it. The first step is to come up with a social media marketing strategy. Once the strategy is in place, you should start informing your audience.

You should focus on growing your business and especially using social media. Provide useful and practical information to your readers. Let them come to trust you on matters that relate to your niche. Continue advising, researching, commenting and producing relevant content and share it with your followers. If you do this regularly, then you can expect to start receiving notifications and requests about your website.

All too often, business owners get on social media and begin asking customers to buy their products or use their services. This kind of approach is ill-advised primarily because your followers do not quite know you. No relationship has developed, and trust has not yet been established. Remember to first give and give some more, and the customers will eventually come calling.

Chapter 1: Building Loyal Customers

Just a couple of years ago, most businesses built customer relations based mostly on face-to-face interactions. However, this no longer applies especially today where plenty of transactions take place online. Even then relationships still have to be maintained. But its harder now to build trust and establish relationships because of problems such as cybercrime and online theft.

Customer loyalty

Customer loyalty is essential if you are to build and establish trust. However, since face to face interactions are no longer there, it is crucial for businesses to learn other ways of establishing loyalty and customer trust. Here are a couple of suggestions.

1. Connect with fans via social media: There is absolutely no doubt that your customers are on social media. Such platforms have been found to be the best places for interacting and communicating with your customers. A lot of consumers use social media to vet a business and see what others think about it. There are plenty of people who get onto social media in order to learn what people are saying about a particular product or service.

2. Provide online customer service: Another excellent way of building customer loyalty is providing customer services online. While most customers are online and not in stores, they still need to interact with and contact businesses. They also require assistance and advice from service providers and all others. Many customers seek help over the internet. If you can provide this service to your customers, then you will be assisting them immensely and strengthening existing relationships.

3. Come up with loyalty programs: One of the best ways of building customer loyalty is to develop and use loyalty programs. About 72% of Europeans and 76%American consumers prefer to shop at stores offering a loyalty program. Such programs are underutilized, yet they are extremely powerful. Customers love to feel wanted and appreciated. Such programs can be offered through free shipping, email coupons, contests, and loyalty points. When you offer such programs, you will have to honor them and not frustrate your customers.

4. Encourage customer reviews and prominently display them: Numerous consumers trust reviews and use them to make decisions about whether or not to purchase a product or use a service. Over 70% of global consumers rely on customer reviews in order to make purchasing decisions. Consumers trust reviews, especially from friends and family. Business owners can take advantage of this to boost the confidence of consumers. Make sure that you encourage customers to post reviews and share their positive experiences with others. When you encourage reviews, you show that you care about your customers' opinion.
Building customer loyalty and trust is essential for any online business that wants to succeed. Customers have numerous options to choose from and will not engage with any businesses that do not make them feel valued. They will also not stay around when they feel their security is threatened. Therefore, take time and implement these simple solutions and customers will then come to trust you and become loyal and faithful to your brand.

Word of Mouth Marketing

One of the most powerful methods of marketing is through word of mouth. This is a powerful tool that works effectively even online. Word of mouth does not just catch people's attention but also gets them talking. Over 62% of consumers seek reviews on the internet before paying for a service or purchasing a product while more than 90% trust brand recommendations from family and friends.

With such numbers, it is crucial that you do not neglect this powerful marketing tool. The recommendations, ratings, and reviews of other customers are crucial when it comes to marketing and customer acquisition.

Think about the person who has a positive experience shopping online and then shares this experience on a platform such as Facebook or Twitter. This is a powerful and organic method of spreading information. Word of mouth marketing is basically a free form of advertising. It refers to personal experiences by customers that are shared with others through different channels.

Word of mouth marketing is also all about creating a buzz. As a brand, you want to gain a following, especially on the various social media. Remember that the more you interact with people then, the more your brand name gets known. This kind of effect is very similar to the snowball effect. Snowballs start small, but as they roll down a hill, they keep getting bigger and bigger.

Some of the tips you can use to implement word-of-mouth marketing include encouraging the use of user-generated content. This is content that is created and shared by consumers. It is usually honest and helps to build trust. It also makes the work of marketers much easier.

Whenever customers leave comments about their positive experiences at your online store, you need to ensure that these are shared across your social media. Testimonials by customers can be written on in video format. You can use platforms such as Crowd, Yelp, and others to share testimonials and comments. You should also seek to get product ratings on your website. Let your customers have the ability to rate or review certain services or products that you are selling.

How to Undertake a Product Launch

Brick and mortar establishments often launch products and services that involve the use of posters, decorating stores with posters, raffles, and giveaways.
The posters often feature the positives of the product or service while some sales representatives will coerce customers into buying the product at a discounted price. However, such tactics are

unsuitable for online businesses. There are other more sophisticated marketing techniques that are suitable for online businesses. There are even frameworks that can guide you on how to launch a product online.

It is advisable to come up with a suitable launch strategy. This is because a launch can signal the beginning of a successful enterprise or a complete flop depending on planning and strategy.

The first step you need to make if you want to launch a product at your online store is to inform consumers about this product. A virtual launch needs to have a website that can take orders from customers and track sales of the products. You should offer discounted prices, offers, coupons and also a way of tracking performance.

Multi-channel approach

It is advisable to launch your products across multiple platforms. Just one platform is not enough. A successful approach should involve producing a viral video, creating teasers, and hosting blogs. It should also involve the use of social media platforms as most customers and followers of different brands are on these platforms. Therefore, when launching a product or a service, think about using multiple channels such as blogs, videos, social media, and so on.

Email marketing

Any well-designed product launch should also include email marketing as part of its strategy. While customers do not necessarily appreciate large amounts of email messages, emails offering samplers of a new product and promotional discounts are always welcome. This is basically an effective method of product promotion. Email marketing should also be used to offer the product at a special discount which may include incentives such as free shipping.

Social media campaigns

Social media is extremely effective when it comes to marketing and advertising your brand. Launching a new product is no different. You need to use a number of effective social media platforms as a launching pad for your products. Think about platforms such as Facebook fan pages, Twitter, and Instagram. Plenty of businesses are switching from print media advertising into the online media. Social media are excellent for most launch functions including interacting with customers, showcasing photos of the product, putting out videos and so on.

Cross-promotion

Another effective approach to product is launch is cross-promotion with other companies. You can find complementary vendors to work with who will undertake the cross-promotion. For example, a business producing skin care products can partner with a company that deals in bath product stores in order to provide amazing deals and discounted offers. In return, you will promote the bath products store and its products on your blogs and other platforms.

Other strategies that you should consider

1. Prelaunch giveaways: If you want your product to take off quickly then you should create an atmosphere of excitement and expectation. To be successful in this, you will need to come up with contests and even free giveaways. Identify a select group of individuals and let them have your product for free in exchange for promoting the product and getting the word out to others.

2. Enhance your organic visibility: Since you already have a website, you will need to optimize it for social media. A website that is optimized for search engines will give you a base of traffic that you can successfully use during the launch and afterward. To optimize your website, you will need to consider things such as a Meta description, keywords, and keyword phrases.

3. Create and share content: One of the most effective and reliable digital marketing strategies is the consistent creation of engaging, captivating, and informative content. This is something you need to keep doing in the medium to long run. You really should spend time creating a high-quality blog that contains useful information which adds value to your readers. The main purpose of the blog and the content you create is to provide your followers with an opportunity to share your content with their friends and followers. This will bring additional readers to your website, and the additional traffic will result in leads and eventually customers.

4. Consider remarketing: You need to have a strategy that understands it is not all about blindly impacting users but also about leading them through the conversion funnel. On your platform and social media profiles, you will have consumers at different stages of the purchase process. Not many consumers will be ready to join you after the initial contact. However, this should not mean that you should abandon them. Instead, stay with them and keep marketing your products to them. If you maintain contact, answer their questions and respond to their comments, you will eventually convert them into customers.

At the same time, you should still maintain contact with your current customers. You do not want them to go away. Therefore, keep in touch with your dedicated customers through social media, through newsletters, and through all other means. And remember to also let them know about any product launches that you plan.

5. Create a recommendation system: Another step that you can include as part of your product launch strategy is a recommendation system. As it is, word of mouth remains a superbly effective means of getting the word out about your products and brand. Most consumers tend to share the products they are using with their friends and family. When they share, you will probably receive more followers and possibly even new customers. Recommendations are definitely a welcome idea.

6. Optimize your website's speeds: There is basically nothing more frustrating than a slow website. When your visitors and customers are unable to load pages, make a purchase, or pay for products, they will definitely abandon your store and find another one. Fixing your website's speeds is a simple thing to do. Customers love websites that work at very fast speeds. A fast and fluid website enhances the customer experience as well as your brand perception. Talk to your website designer or service provider as they will be able to easily fix this for you.

7. Establish a relationship with bloggers: Digital marketing strategies are currently led by influencers. Many of them have their own blogs and command huge followings across different social media channels. This loyal following is willing and ready to listen to the influencer and follow their direction or recommendation. If you want the attention of influencers and bloggers, then you may have to pay them to promote your products and brand.

Alternatively, you could hold an event such as a launch and then send free samples to these influencers and bloggers. They will review the products and write reviews on their social media pages and blogs. However, they are very loyal to their followers and will never recommend something that they do not approve. Be sure to check out influencers in different niches before engaging their services. Try and identify which bloggers are best suited for your products and which ones are not. This way, you will be able to focus on a winner rather than take chances with one who stands little chance.

You can also nudge them to get the process started. This is easy as you can always offer an incentive. Simply create a system for recommendations where you reward any of your followers or customers who recommend your brand and products. People generally love free things so offer a free product or discounted offer if they share information about your product with their followers or friends and family.

Chapter 2: Where is your Audience Mostly?

As a business owner, it is crucial that you understand the different social media audience demographics. By doing this, you will be able to better select your social media channels and also improve your marketing.

Social media is absolutely important for any online business. However, there are numerous social media platforms out there. You have social networking websites such as Facebook, Twitter, Pinterest, LinkedIn, YouTube and many others. Each has its own kind of audience. For instance, users on platforms such as LinkedIn are a little different from those on Facebook and Instagram. This can make marketing a real challenge because of not knowing the most ideal platform to use.

Marketing on each social media is also pretty tough. It is a time-consuming exercise, yet the efforts may not necessarily pay off. Businesses and brands need to know which platforms are worth prioritizing so they can market themselves appropriately. This is why it is crucial to understand who is where and on what platforms are most of your customers. The knowledge will enhance your Facebook advertising and Instagram marketing techniques.

Do your research

It is well worth your time to research and find out who your right audience is and on what social media channels they are on. You need to think about the kind of audiences you need to reach on social media. You need to ask yourself a couple of questions. For instance, who is interested in your products and on what social media platforms are they? What can you do in order to appeal to a particular kind of audience?

Another question that you need to ask is what kind of platforms are your audiences on? First of all, you need to understand and appreciate the power of word of mouth marketing. This is a powerful marketing technique that works extremely well especially on social media. Your customers on social media are likely to talk about their experiences with a product or a service and then share this information with others. It is important to follow and connect with followers that are already connected to your target audience.

Demographics

Now your audiences and followers are not just a bunch of random people. They work in certain industries and sectors of the economy. Your audience lies within a certain age range and showcases a certain personality trait. Some love using social media while others are tech savvy. As a business owner and online marketing strategist, you need to do your research well and understand the demographics of your audience.

The best approach is to start by first segmenting your audience. This is easy if you start by creating follower profiles. Keep a record of this and use a spreadsheet to make things easier. Once you have the data that you need, keep the record and then analyze to find out what you come up with. It is possible that some unexpected outcome may result. Make sure that you keep updating this spreadsheet and keep improving your results.

Work with key influencers

Another step that you need to take is to identify influencers within your niche that you can work with. There are influencers on major social media sites with huge followings. They have dedicated followers who listen to them and follow their lead. Influencers generally stand out within a given community and others tend to listen to them. They include stakeholders within a given niche, thought leaders, journalists, and peers. Basically, they are individuals who challenge the ordinary and offer game-changing ideas and opinions.

Typical audiences

Some of your typical audiences that you will be searching for include the following individuals and groups of people;

- Your current customers or clients
- Potential customers or clients
- Associates of both current and potential clients or customers
- Editors and journalists
- Bloggers and influencers
- Affiliate businesses
- And thought leaders

Sometimes it is easy to pick these individuals and professionals out, but at other times you may need assistance. Fortunately, there are plenty of free monitoring tools that you can use. These tools can track down individuals mentioning keywords relevant to your business and niche.

Some of these tools include Board Reader, Social Mention, and Google Analytics. These will easily highlight the most crucial and most important voices in your niche area. Once these individuals have been profiled, you will need to track them down. Identifying them and then contacting them is a process that can take some time. You will have to find out which particular social media to use. So how will you do this? The solution will vary based upon your target audience.

Fortunately, you have access to information that can help to guide you through this process. There is insightful data available that shows you which demographics are found on which social media websites.

Facebook

Just about everyone is on Facebook. It is the world's largest social media platform, and most major brands and businesses have a presence here. As a business owner trying to promote your brand and gain new followers, you really have to be on this platform.

There are hundreds of millions of account holders on Facebook with more than 2 billion monthly users. Most users visit the website approximately every single day. Since Facebook is such a large website, it is safe to assume that most people have an account. However, there are certain clear trends that showcase the most active groups.

- Basically, women use Facebook a lot more than men. Over 83% of women are on Facebook while only 75% of men have accounts. This basically means you are able to reach both demographics even though you can reach more women than men.

- Most age groups are well represented on Facebook. This social media website represents just about all age demographics. Even then, most users or members are between the ages of 18 to 29. About 88% of young people in this age group are on Facebook. About 84% of individuals aged 30 to 49 have accounts, 72% of people aged between 50 and 64 years and about 62% of those aged over 65 years. It is only kids aged between 13 and 17 years who mostly prefer socializing on Snapchat.

- Most users on Facebook are college educated with a reasonable income. About 77% of people who claim to have attended or graduated college are on Facebook. This compares to about 56% of those who completed high school without attending college. Also, plenty of users on the platform earn at least $75,000 or more annually.

Twitter

Twitter is very popular when it comes to marketing. While it does not have a following as large as that of Facebook, it is very influential. It is said that at least 66% of users have discovered a brand or product on the site. Also, over 69% of users have made a purchase on the website based on content that they came across on the platform.

It is a platform where numerous brands should consider having a presence. Twitter has about 350 million users each month. These users visit the site almost every day. Basically, about 43% visit the website on a daily basis while about 24% visit the platform at least once a week.

Who is on Twitter? A lot of the demographics on Twitter are similar to those on Facebook. The main difference between the two platforms is that 21% of both women and men are on Twitter. Here are some more demographics about Twitter;

- *The most active demographics are young people:* Individuals aged between 18 and 29 are the most active on Twitter. Twitter users within this age bracket constitute about 36% of all users. Those between the ages of 30 to 49 years constitute about 22% followed by 18% of those aged between 50 and 64 years old. Only 6% of users are aged 65 years and above.

- *Most users have an advanced education and high incomes:* Just as with Facebook, a majority of users have high incomes with most users also claiming at least higher education qualifications.

- *There is a large international audience on the platform:* There is a huge presence of Twitter users who dwell outside the United States. More than 79% of users reside in places outside the USA with a majority of them based in Japan, Brazil, and Mexico. Twitter is, therefore, suitable for business owners seeking to sell to international buyers.

Instagram

The most popular social media website after Facebook has got to be Instagram. This social networking site lays a claim on 28% of the population. The site is used mainly to share photos, images, and videos rather than information. Even then the site attracts a huge number of users and has reportedly registered a huge number of engagements compared to almost all other platforms.

Instagram demographics

Instagram has more than 600 million users with active accounts. More than half of all users access their accounts at least every day while about 25% visit the website at least once each week.

A lot of the demographics are similar to those on Facebook and other platforms. Even then, there are plenty of young users on Instagram. They constitute the majority of users, and they spend a lot of time sharing visual content including videos and photos. These users are not just young but educated and trendy.

There are more female than male users on Instagram: This is the case not just on Instagram but on other platforms such as Facebook and Snapchat. However, the difference is larger here than elsewhere. More than 32% of women claim to have an Instagram account compared to only 23% of men.

Users are from all income brackets: Instagram users are from different income brackets. While there are some notable differences when it comes to percentages, the distribution is generally the same across the brackets. This is unlike the demographics on sites like Facebook where most users are middle- and high-income earners.

A lot of international users: Instagram boasts of a large international base of users. Just like Facebook and Twitter, there are plenty of users from around the globe. You can use Instagram as a perfect launching pad of selling to international customers.

After all, over 80% of Instagram users reside outside the United States.

LinkedIn

LinkedIn is a professional networking website. It is slightly different from other social networks in that it is more about professionals and businesses. However, it shares a number of demographic trends with other popular social networking websites. It is especially useful for businesses seeking to engage other businesses or B2B networking. Your advertising and marketing efforts will fare very well on this platform.

LinkedIn users

There are over 500 million users on LinkedIn. This mark was attained early in 2017. However, as this is a business network, users do not visit it as often as they should. At least when compared to other social networking sites. Only 18% of the 500 million users visit the website on a daily basis. About 31% visit only once a week. Most of all the other users claim to visit the site fewer times than that.

Demographics

It is easy to assume that LinkedIn is full of older people and less activity compared to other networking sites. However, this is not necessarily accurate. There are plenty of younger individuals on this platform. For instance, over 39% of LinkedIn users are aged between 18 and 29 years. Those aged between 30 and 49 years old constitute about 31% of users while 21% are aged between 50 and 64 years.

High levels of higher educated individuals: As expected, LinkedIn has a high number of highly educated individuals and professionals. More than half the members are college graduates. Those with some college education are at least 25%, and those with a high school education are about 9%.

High-income individuals: Members on LinkedIn are also well-paid individuals. Close to 50% of members earn at least $75,000 annually while only 23% earn less than $30,000.

Gender: There are more male users on this social network compared to all others. In fact, this is one of the very few social networking websites with more men than women. However, the difference is not that large. Twenty-eight percent of men have accounts on LinkedIn while only 23% of women have active profiles on the website.

Pinterest

The social networking site Pinterest is now considered among the major social media websites. It boasts a whopping 150 million users and is popular among business owners and individuals alike. The site has managed to achieve quite a lot considering that it only emerged in 2010.

Pinterest used to be huge with foodies and brides-to-be. Today, however, it is a lot more than just a database for recipes and wedding photos. There are numerous images on the website including 75 billion ideas that aptly represent all types of content and users. These users range from millennials to music experts, college professors, students, career civil servants, and even servicemen and women.

Most people used to visit Pinterest to get ideas about various issues and matters. Today however users are visiting the site to shop and view images. And they do really shop on this website. According to a recent study, more than 87% of pinners on the website have purchased something they saw on the website and a whopping 93% plan to do so in the near future.

Demographics

The majority of users on Pinterest are female even though an increasing number of men are beginning to show interest in this site. This is according to a Pew Research study conducted in 2016 of online US-based adults. The study revealed that about 45% of women use Pinterest compared to only 17% of men.

Some of the most popular goods and niches that are of great interest to women on the platform include clothing, home décor, and food. Women also use Pinterest for other purposes such as finding ideas they can use and planning for their futures. Forty-seven percent of users on the website were likely planning for a life event such as a wedding or buying a home or even a trip.

Pinterest is popular with followers of all ages. We have millennials, baby boomers and Generation X all well represented. However, millennials constitute the largest demographic at 36% of all Pinterest users. These are users between the ages of 18 to 29. Baby boomers or people aged between 50 to 65 years constitute 18% of all users on the platform. Therefore, as a business owner or marketer, if you want to target millennials, then Pinterest is a social website that you should consider. There is a good reason for this. Basically, 47% of all millennials on the site have purchased something compared to online 9% on Facebook and 14% on Twitter.

Millennials really do rely on Pinterest to get ideas on what to buy. For instance, over 80% of all millennials on the site while 72% use the pin-board provided on the network to connect with preferred brands. Another 71% logon to the website to find products they need to purchase. This goes to show how crucial this website is to millennials and what a valuable demographic they are for marketers.

Finding your Audience on Social Media

Now that you have a better understanding of the various social media and where your potential customers are, the next step is to actually find out where they really are. When it comes to finding your target audience on the various social networking sites, you need to have a suitable strategy.

First, you need to think about who you need to contact and engage with. To do this successfully, you will need to think beyond the obvious. Think, for instance, who would be interested in your service or products? Take some time and think about these people. Where are they likely to hang out? What age ranges are they? Which social media platforms do they prefer and are they tech-savvy? You need to ask yourself these and numerous other questions. As soon as the answers begin to stream in, you need to take notes and segment these people. They will eventually constitute your customer base across various social media platforms.

Finding people on Twitter

It is easy to search for people on Twitter. The URL www.search.twitter.com is a great place to begin your Twitter search. Use this tool to search for your followers including their locations and demographics. It can help you identify the influencers in your niche and then browse their followers.

You can also use "Twitterrel" to identify and track down users discussing topics related to your industry. You should also make use of relevant hashtags used for particular events or occasions. It is possible to come across excellent people on various hashtags.

Finding people on LinkedIn

LinkedIn is even easier to use. All that you need to do is search for an individual by their name. There is a search box available that you can use to conduct your search. The same search box can be used to search for relevant keywords that will help you find exactly what you are looking for.

During your searches try and use "and" plus "or" if you wish to use multiple keywords. This way, you will be able to search a number of words or each term individually across profiles. It is also possible to search for users using their email addresses. A good idea would be to join a relevant group such as one that is affiliated with your industry or niche.

Finding people on Facebook

You can use Facebook to find people using your email address. Therefore, if you already have an email address of followers, potential leads, and customers, then you can easily find them on Facebook. You can also search for fan pages on Facebook that are relevant to your industry and niche then check out the fans there.

Try and find some key influencers and then check out who their followers are. Connect with more and more people this way because these are your possible customers. Remember to use filters when using the search engines so that you narrow down your search to the kind of followers you want.

Remember that finding followers or customers is a process and not an event. It is something you will keep doing for a while until you have a reasonable following. Therefore, keep searching and keep adding more and more friends and do this consistently for a while.

Tips and advice for business owners and marketers

Always place more focus on social media websites that closely represent your main target audience. There are no distinct social media platforms that completely represent a certain demographic but there us an overlap. You will probably have to select three of four platforms to start with before adding on some more. Having a presence in most of them is crucial, but you do not have to be on all popular social media. Therefore, learn how to prioritize on the best social media to be on.

Focus on audiences on the various platforms and then proceed to target them with suitable or appropriate marketing initiatives. You need to keep in mind that each platform is different therefore ensure that your approach is tailored to each social media's strengths and the kind of audience you are targeting.

Ensure that you create messages that appeal to your audiences, so they feel compelled to listen to you and follow you.

Make use of analytics

Analytics are extremely important because they will provide you with information that you can use. You will receive crucial data as well as an understanding about what is working, who your most loyal followers are, what your customers' demographics are and so much more. This information will enable you to adjust your approach and use methods and processes that actually work and produce results.

You also need to really ignore the larger audience on your preferred platforms. Instead, focus a lot more on your chosen niche and industry and try to capitalize on this specific audience. Remember that social media marketing is pretty competitive because almost all other businesses are also here. Even then, you should mostly focus on your audience and ensure that your efforts are targeted at them. As a brand, you need to always strive for targeted and focused initiatives in order to acquire the results that you desire.

Chapter 3: Customer and Competition Research

As a business owner, you know that you should research your customers as well as your competition. This is because the insights from your research will greatly enhance your marketing strategy and enable you to reach out to even more followers and customers.

However, most people are unaware of how exactly to conduct this research. As a small business or even a startup, you really should learn how to research your potential customers. You should also find out where you need to begin and the kind of useful details you should add to your potential customers.

How well do you know your customer?

It is important that you get to know your customers very well. For instance, you need to find out who they are, what their education levels are, their annual incomes, and the problems that they want to be solved. It is crucial that you also understand some basic details such as how they like their coffee.

There are many reasons why you need to know your customer and understand more about him. According to a recent survey, about 34% of consumers said they broke up with a brand simply because of an irrelevant, disruptive, or poor message. This is a clear indication that companies probably do not understand their customers and do not even bother to research about them.

You need to keep in mind that knowing your customer is more than just guesswork. The ideal situation is to put yourself in their shoes. Find out what their problems, issues, questions, and challenges are. To really understand them, you need to conduct some serious research on your customers. Some of the most effective approaches include one-on-one conversations. These could be via the phone, over a cup of coffee and perhaps even on Skype.

Get on Google Forums

One of the most reliable platforms to learn more about your customers is Google Forum. Google allows people to open groups and then discuss their own personal matters and affairs on them. Business owners can start groups, and their followers or customers can join and leave comments or join discussions.

There are numerous groups as well as discussion forums available. As a business owner, you can log onto these platforms and see what consumers are saying about your industry. It is crucial to spend a bit of time on these forums. Apparently, not many people do this, so you stand a great chance of obtaining useful information. This information can then be used to come up with a better marketing strategy as well as improved products and better services. Find customers within your range and then read the forums and learn about what they are saying. Many will express their problems and challenges. Others will speak about possible solutions. Listen to all these opinions, try and understand where they are coming from, and join in with possible solutions. If they think that you are adding value to their lives by providing solutions, then you will even be able to gain a few more followers and possible customers.

Find blogs related to your niche

You should also search for blogs related to your industry or your niche. Such blogs are often written by industry insiders or experts. They are not just a wealth of information but also a magnet for consumers and others interested in the niche. If you come across blogs with hundreds of comments, take your time to read some of the most prominent comments. These are the ones with the highest number of responses or activity such as likes. Note the author of the comment and see if you can get them to follow you on social media.

Also, try and join in the conversation. Present yourself as an industry insider who has solutions to the problems of the readers.

Even as you provide detailed solutions for free, you should find ways of redirecting the consumers to your website. Do this by adding a link to your answer directing readers to your site for further information.

The information that you gather at such a forum is crucial and will provide crucial insights which you can use to better your marketing strategies and improve your customer service and products. Take time to analyze the comments and understand the problems and issues that your potential customers need addressed.

Mix your Sources and Research Methods

At the end of your research and survey, you want to ensure the entire process consists of a balanced quantitative and qualitative research by making use of both secondary and primary sources of information. You need to ensure that when you research a subject, your goal is not simply to get a grip on the statistical group profile but to also appreciate the not-so-obvious nuances of an individual customer as well as their thought process.

There are a couple of simple steps that can get you started with the research process. These will help you to get you started. You can do your research offline and also online. There are various methods available to assist you with both approaches. Below are a couple of easy but effective methods of learning more about your prospects. Some methods require some financial resources while others do not.

Use Talk Walker Alerts, Mention, and Google Alerts

As a business owner or marketer, you need to leverage plenty of information that is available online. This is one way of accessing information about your customers and prospective buyers. One way of doing this is through the site www.google.com/alerts. You can use this site to create an alert for each customer behavior or company then select notification frequency that you prefer. The frequency could be once a day, a couple of times each day, once every two days and so on.

However, Google is not the only website providing this service. There are others who are perhaps even more reliable. There is Mention at www.en.mention.com, and there is Talk Walker Alerts at the URL address www.talkwater.com/alerts. These two websites do a whole lot more compared to Google Alerts as they monitor obscure blogs and social networking websites.

Once you select your preferred site, make sure that you preview the results. This will ensure that you have your parameters correctly set. Should you be trying to monitor a business or a public company, then you will quickly find out about their activities, interests, and initiatives. If you are monitoring the activities of technology consumers, then an instant alert will inform should any relevant news get published.

Also, if you are trying to sell your products and promote your brand, then you will be able to easily monitor useful trends as well as specific prospects and actual customers. These trends will provide you with so much useful information and data that will help you achieve your marketing aims.

Conduct interviews with some of your current customers

An interview with your current customers may seem a little too obvious, but most business owners hardly spend much time talking to their buyers. Your customers are the perfect resource that you need because they have bought products from you or paid for your services and are also easily accessible to you.

Therefore, take the time to speak with your customers and hold interviews with them where possible. Through the interviews, you will get insights into their decision-making process. You will also gain useful content that you will need for any case studies. If you and your customer agree to jointly prepare and promote a case study, then you will both emerge victorious.

You can also conduct a survey in addition to customer interviews. You also have the option of holding or conducting focus group discussions with prospective customers. The main purpose here is to find out what these prospects have in common, what their main sources of information are and also what are some of the challenges they encounter. However, you need to keep in mind that each customer is unique especially for professional services firms. It is sometimes tempting to project the views of one business onto another. This can very likely lead you astray. It is advisable to learn about how to minimize the risk of misusing customer demographics.

Closely study your web analytics

Your web analytics provide you with tons of data which you can use to gain information about your customers. However, you need to first ask yourself some pertinent questions if you are to successfully use this data. For instance, you can ask yourself the following questions;

- What keywords did your customers use to find you?
- What are your visitors' patterns of behavior?
- Where are the visitors from?
- What part of your website did they visit?
- How long do they stay on each page?
- What content format is considered most important?
- Are you able to understand where your customers are along the purchase process?

This information can be utilized to improve your landing pages and website in order to attract more prospects that are interested in your brand and products. This information is also useful if you are considering adopting an inbound marketing system.

Check out your competitors

Another method of acquiring useful information and insights into your potential customers is to check out your competitors. What you need to do is to study the case studies or research published by your competitors. When you review your competitors' case studies, you will get better insights into your prospective customers and the reasons why they chose your competitor instead of your business. Also, apart from just following your competition, you should also follow industry reports and analyst blogs.

Leverage professional social networks

There are large professional networking websites such as Quora and LinkedIn. There are probably plenty of other industry-specific or niche-specific networking websites out there. Try and search for those that are relevant to your niche.

These networks are excellent as they provide you with a huge opportunity for engaging and listening t professionals. You will be able to better understand the frequent challenges and successes of your potential customers. Through these networks, you can ask questions and inquire about additional problems and any solutions they think might be suitable.

You will get an opportunity to ask questions among community members and acquire truly thoughtful and real responses. You will be able to enhance your data that is already in your possession and see how it connects with other people that you know or those who own their own businesses.

Researching your Customers

If you are to successfully know your customers and understand them, then you need to research them. One of the most effective ways of doing this is through personal interviews. This could be one-on-one sessions, discussions over the phone and sometimes on Skype. Such discussions offer some of the most effective ways of getting into your customer's head.

The main challenge is that this method is not scalable should you wish to collect data from a large group of consumers. It is also time-consuming and hence the need for an online solution. Online research can assist with the information gathering process to ensure that you receive the kind of feedback from customers in order to improve your business practices and create better products for them.

Whenever you get online, you need to listen to your customers and generally members within your industry or niche. Therefore, identify the relevant platforms or websites where your customers are likely to be. Some of them include Quora at www.quora.com.

1. Quora

One of the best websites to conduct your research is Quora. This is because this site is full of individuals holding serious conversations and discussions about topical issues and generally a broad range of topics. These can range from immigration to politics to food and so on. All you need to do in order to get started is to enter a keyword into the search query box. The system will serve a list of different conversations featuring your preferred keywords. You can expect one or more of these conversations to reveal what your customers are thinking and how this affects your business.

2. Blog comments

There are different ways of researching using blog comments. For a business owner with a successful blog full of reader comments across different blog posts, you will gain insightful data or information about your market's main problems, issues, and concerns.

There are blogs on the internet that receive hundreds of comments each year. Blog owners often encourage their readers to leave comments and share their thoughts. Such comments provide the blog writer or owner with a wealth of information about what the readers are thinking.

If you do not have your own blog, then consider checking out other blogs within the industry. It is possible to find information pertaining to your niche across various blogs. Therefore, check out different blogs and search for common threads. You can find a particular topic, search across different industry blogs and see what consumers are saying. These comments provide a wealth of information that you can use.

3. Surveys

Another great option that you can use to gather information and thoughts about your customers is the use of surveys. There are long-form surveys often used by businesses to gather information. Surveys are excellent for online customer research. You first need to create a survey and then load it onto one of the popular survey platforms such as Survey Monkey, www.surveymonkey.com. As soon as the survey is ready, all you need to do is send a link to your contacts. You probably have a list of email addresses from your customers. Make use of this mailing list to send out the survey.

If you want the survey to have a high uptake, make sure you offer an incentive. This could be something simple but worthwhile such as a Starbucks gift card or even the chance to win a prize. Sometimes companies even offer to pay individuals who complete surveys. Survey companies like Survey Monkey and others offer to find people that fit your preferred demographics.

Yet another approach that you can use is the short pop-up survey that appears suddenly right at the bottom of a user's website. There are application programs that can help with this such as "Qualaroo" at www.qualaroo.com. You can use this particular approach to confirm a common belief or to test product ideas for your target market. Remember to keep these short surveys as brief as possible. If you can stick to just one question, then you will be alright.

Social media research

One of the most effective ways of researching your customers is through the various social media. It is a fact that social media is a trove of free data about your customers that you can use. If you have access to the right kind of tools, then you can find out a lot about your customers. For instance, you will learn about what questions they are asking and what kind of content they are sharing.

Once you understand this kind of information, you will be able to understand what kind of problems they are facing which will enable you to come up with a solution to their problems. You will also be in a position to define your content and your social media strategies. As a business owner, it is crucial that you learn how to quickly conduct social media research and put the outcome into practice.

Get onto different social networking sites

Your customers are on some of the most popular social media sites including Facebook, Instagram, Twitter, YouTube, and all the others. You will most likely find pages related to your industry on these social platforms. Join these pages and also follow industry leaders. Check out the main posts and the major commentators and influence leaders.

Find out the questions that your customers are asking

Your customers probably have certain challenges, questions, and problems that they are faced with. They often express these questions and challenges on different social media, sharing with others undergoing similar predicaments. If you can join the conversations and provide a solution, you will be able to acquire new customers and address their questions even as you support existing ones. And while at it you should also outline your content strategy which addresses their questions and challenges.

The best solutions that you provide are those that generally address their problems. This means providing practical and useful solutions that actually address the problems that your audience has. You should ensure that your business is structured or modeled to provide solutions to your customers.

You need to note that the best products solve problems and address customers' issues. As such, if you are able to solve a problem with the solutions that you provide, then your customers are more likely to trust you as an expert and buy your products. You can use the following tools to help you with your research.

- Twitter Search
- LinkedIn Answers
- Twitter
- Pinterest
- Facebook Search

Research your competition

Regardless of your industry or niche, you will always have competition. Remember that there are other businesses selling the same products and probably to the same customer base as you. It is possible to check out social media websites in order to find your competition.

Social media users are generally free to choose their preferred social media platforms. They are also free to follow anyone and choose their preferred content to read or consume. Therefore, if you want to attract users to your page, then you have to create content that meets the needs and desires of your users. Ideally, you need to find out which content types work best for them and which ones are not suitable at all.

To learn about your customers' or followers' preferred content types, you will need to learn more about your competitors. There are several ways of researching the competition, and one of them is through social media analytics. Basically, most of your competitors are on various social media, so it is advisable to use the different social media tools in order to track them down.

1. Set up a social media campaign

Let us say you own a business that provides delivery services to pet owners. You specialize in delivering pet food. Such a niche definitely has serious competition. If you want to stand out and outperform your competition, then you have to find out what they are doing wrong and improve on it. You can also perform better where they are performing just right.

Setting up the tools that you need in order to find out more about your competition is really fast and easy. These tools will enable you to compare social media strategies so that you learn what your competitor is up to. If you know the competitors, then that will be easy for you but if you don't then you will need to search and find them.

2. Search across different social media websites

We already know which the top social media websites are. These include Facebook, Twitter, YouTube, Instagram, Snapchat, LinkedIn, Quora, and many others. There are search bars on most of these social websites. Use the search bar as well as other tools provided in order to track down your competition.

When you finally track them down, you will need to read their posts and see what their followers and customers are saying. Try and find out what problems the followers are talking about as well as their challenges. You can also try and identify who the influential followers are and what they are saying to their followers.

You can also place an order from your competition and find out more about their products and services. You will learn about the cost of the products, their shipping times, the kind of after-sales

46

services offered and so much more. This will help you come up with your own strategy.

Do this for about 10 of your main competitors. These are probably businesses operating within your niche and selling to customers that you want to sell to. When you finally find information from most of your competitors, you should analyze it and find out what they are doing wrong and where they are excelling. With this information, you should then be able to come up with an excellent strategy. When you combine all the different ideas from your main competitors, you should now be able to come up with the ultimate social media plan for your business.

Chapter 4: Marketing

The Basics of Social Media Marketing

The average person spends about an hour and a half each day on social media. This amounts to 28% of the time we spend on the internet. This is a significant amount of time considering we run our businesses over the internet and do all other things such as read the mail, pay some bills, do internet banking, and catch up with the news.

Social media marketing

Social media marketing is a crucial aspect of our online businesses. If you get it right, then it will be an endlessly profitable process that will bring in the customers and plenty of money. As a business owner, you need to understand the benefits of understanding and investing in social media marketing.

Social media marketing will help you to promote events, announce new products to your audience, create brand awareness, develop a community of followers and customers, drive leads and sales as well as increase website traffic. This process generally relies on transparency and authenticity.

Getting started

Once you are ready to get started, there are a couple of steps that you should take. These steps provide an excellent opportunity for you to get started. Here they are in the correct order;

1. Determine the goals you wish to optimize for: There are plenty of things that you may wish to promote via social media. It could be your brand, a new product, promote your business and so on.

2. Identify the platforms that suit your business the best: If you are just starting out, then you should start small to enable you to handle the communities across the different social media. You definitely need to get started with Facebook. The second social media site will depend on your business. If you have tangible products, then consider opening an Instagram page.

3. Create a content schedule: As a business owner on social media, you will need to keep your followers and customers engaged. The best approach is to provide your readers with fresh content on a regular basis. In order to get this right, you need to come up with a schedule. You should ideally post between 4 to 7 times each week depending on social media site. On sites such as Twitter, you will have to post almost daily. On others such as Facebook, 3 to 4 times each week is sufficient. Fortunately, there are application programs that can help you to manage this schedule. Think about Agora Pulse at www.agorapulse.com. This website has a content calendar which will post content for you and help with everything else.

4. Source curated content: As a business owner, you are probably busy and may not be able to come up with all the cool content needed for your social media campaigns. Fortunately, you can always search for curated content all across the internet. Share this content with your followers across different platforms.

5. Monitor all your platforms: Always be actively engaged on your social media platforms and observe what kind of relative content within your industry or niche is out there. Also, make sure that you keep engaging your followers and customers. Answer their questions, respond to their comments, and generally get engaged. It is important that you do not ignore your followers or else they may leave.

- *Get fully engaged on social media*

There are plenty of businesses just like yours trying to get onto social media. As such, you cannot afford to just have a presence. Instead, you really should actively participate. If you seek to only exist, then you will lose the huge advantage that social media affords businesses.

As an example, about 30% of all millennials on social media engage with a brand at least once each month. Having a presence on different social media will enable you to interact with customers from across the various demographics and help you to gain more customers and increase your profits. Here are some ways of creating a successful social media marketing strategy.

- *Come up with social media market goals*

One of the things that you need to consider as you open social media pages for your brand is to have goals that address some of your biggest challenges. Remember that social media marketing doesn't simply mean checking and checking out. Instead, it should be viewed as a serious event and a major aspect of your overall marketing strategy. Basically, you need to set goals and ensure that all the goals that you set are achievable. If you come up with achievable goals, then you are more likely to be successful in pursuing them.

Also, remember to only have a presence on certain relevant social media in order not to complicate your marketing strategy. You should find only those channels that are suitable for your strategy to avoid over-complicating things. Having a simple approach can take you really far.

Document your social media goals. This is advisable to ensure that you can benchmark and also increase your chances of successfully achieving them. There is strong evidence that suggests those who write down their goals are 30 times more successful compared to those who don't. Some of the goals that you can set to achieve in 2019 may include some of the following;

- Increase your brand awareness
- Improve the quality of sales of your business
- Improve your ROI or return on investment
- Create a loyal fan base
- Keep an eye on the competition

- *Research your social media audience*

It is said that almost 80% of all adults are on Facebook and log in regularly to catch up with friends and generally interact with others. It is crucial that you research and understand your audience. This is necessary so that you find out exactly who your customers are, what their ages are, their income levels, and all other kinds of information.

- *Engage your audience and do NOT ignore them*

Social networking websites are designed for engagements. All the people who use social media do so in order to discuss, share, converse, and generally engage with other users.
As a business owner, you cannot afford to ignore these crucial followers. Your audience is really important. It is from this following that you will get your leads, traffic to your website and even customers. Therefore, answer their questions, respond to their queries, share their content and basically engage with them in any way possible.

Also, remember to post your content at the best times possible. There are times that are ideal for posting on most social sites. Find out what the best times are for your preferred channels and then post your content at these times. You should also ensure that you have a community manager ready to respond to posts and questions from your followers.

- *Keep track of your efforts*

As a business owner, you should keep a close eye on your social media performance. Analyzing your efforts and checking out your metrics is important. You should analyze your efforts and monitor your performance so that you understand what strategies work and what approaches need improvement. It is crucial to generally be on the lookout on the performance of your social media pages at all times.

- *Consistency*

As a business owner, you need to ensure consistency across all your social media pages. For instance, you need to ensure that your "About Us" page and your social media Home Pages have the same cover photos and usernames. This kind of consistency gives you credibility and tells your followers that you can be trusted. It is also easy to recognize your pages from one social media site to another.

If you are on Instagram, then you should ensure that you have a daily story. Instagram users appreciate fresh content provided on a regular basis. Make sure that you share this story on your Facebook page as well. This should be easy as these two sites are interconnected.

- *Listed*

You should get listed on all your social media pages so that your customers can search for you and actually find you. It is important that your followers, customers, and all others are able to find you when they search for you. If they cannot find your page, then they most likely will find someone else.

- *Provide useful content*

As a business owner with followers across different social media platforms, you should take time to develop useful content that adds value to your followers or audience.

Your audience and followers have certain problems and issues which are common within your industry. As a business owner, you need to research what these problems are and then find solutions. Provide content and answer these questions the best way that you can.

Your aim here is to answer the questions that your viewers have. Do this regularly across different platforms. Let them eventually get to trust you as an authority on those specific issues. If they begin to trust you, then you can redirect them to your blogs and websites. From here on you can groom your followers into paying customers. The principle here is very simple. First, give, give, and then give some more before you eventually start receiving. This principle works perfectly all the time.

Use apps to post your content

As a business owner, you are probably busy attending to your customers and business most of the day. You probably lack the time to develop and post content on social media on a regular basis. Just the knowledge that you have to develop content for each of your social media accounts can be daunting.

The good news is that you do not have to break your back developing fresh content every day. There are plenty of apps that can help with this. One of them is Muse Cam. This is an application that helps you to shoot great images on the iOS platform. The images can then be edited using advanced tools and other features.

You can also use an app known as Boomerang. This is an application that takes a series of great images in quick succession. The effect is to create a GIF-like image that you can then share on your various social media platforms. There are plenty of other tools that can actually schedule your social media content posting for an entire week or so. This saves you the time and effort of having to log onto each of your social media platforms in order to post and share content.

Guerilla Marketing

The term guerrilla marketing may conjure up images of rebellion and conflict. However, when it comes to marketing, this is not the case. When this concept is applied to marketing, it takes on a different meaning.

Guerilla marketing is a type of marketing and advertising strategy that focuses on low-cost strategies that provide maximum yields. Many marketers view guerilla marketing as an extremely unconventional form of marketing which, however, is very effective. Due to its unconventional nature, guerrilla marketing is not easy to explain but is best understood when observed.

Alternative advertising

Guerilla marketing is a form of alternative advertising. It differs from mainstream advertising and is preferred because of its relatively low cost as well as effectiveness in getting the message out.

The aim of this form of marketing is to take the customer by complete surprise. The advertising messages have a much more powerful impact on consumers compared to traditional ads. This is largely because guerrilla ads aim to affect the consumer at a more memorable and personal level.

Guerilla marketing tactics

Guerrilla marketing adverts are much more suitable for small businesses seeking to advertise to a large base of consumers but without the budget to do so. Sometimes large corporations also use this marketing approach, especially when conducting grassroots campaigns. However, they do so to complement their other marketing campaigns. Individuals have also adapted guerrilla marketing tactics. They use this approach when they seek to find more work or to get noticed in a crowd.

Large businesses

While this particular marketing tactic is ideal for small businesses with limited budgets, many large corporations are adopting it. Their budgets are already large, and brands established. Even then, they prefer guerrilla marketing tactics to enhance their overall marketing strategy.

However, such approaches are risky when adapted by big businesses. In some cases, these tactics have been known to collapse, and flop miserably. When this happens, it becomes a total PR nightmare for the companies involved, and they have to readjust their strategies. Fortunately, small businesses stand no such risks and are able to engage in guerrilla marketing successfully.

Guerilla marketing, and small businesses

If you own a small business, then guerilla marketing may be the ideal marketing strategy. The reason is that, if you have a good ad, and execute it well, then the effect will be far reaching while the cost will be relatively low. Guerrilla ads provide an excellent way of getting noticed and help to distinguish you from the competition.

Budget-friendly ads

Guerrilla marketing is a favorite with small business owners because it is an affordable approach to advertising. What is essential is actually coming up with a catchy, creative ad that is well thought-out, and well presented. The ad implementation does not have to be costly, but creativity is also necessary here. Guerilla marketing is seen as a type of time investment rather than financial.

Types of guerilla marketing

There are different types of guerrilla marketing. While these are very few, it is good to learn about them, and see how they apply in real life situations. Yes this is a Social Media Marketing Guide however this does not mean you ignore other way of gaining extra traffic to stay ahead of everyone else!

1. Outdoor guerrilla marketing: This type of approach makes use of existing street furniture or anything out on the street. For instance, a marketer can place a temporary advertising message onto a statue, a park bench, street light, and so on. Even artworks will do. These can be strategically placed on sidewalks or walls across streets.

2. Indoor guerilla marketing: This type of guerrilla advertising is very similar to the indoor guerrilla marketing. The only difference is that this type takes place outdoors in places such as a railway station, university campuses, and shops. It is just as effective as the ads are personal and targeted at individuals.

3. Event ambush guerilla marketing: People do attend events, and sometimes in great numbers. If you have a relevant product or provide a related service, then you can leverage this audience especially in the process of the event. It could be a sporting event or a convert or any other. This doesn't really matter. However, take the opportunity presented by the event to market, and promote your product. Do this in a noticeable way and without necessarily seeking permission from the program organizers or sponsors.

4. Experiential guerrilla marketing: This approach includes all of the above examples. The only difference is that it calls for interactions with viewers or audience. Audience members will, in this case, be expected to interact with the brand for maximum effect.

Approaches to creating guerrilla ads

First, identify the most pressing problem that your products or service solves. Now be creative and think about the kinds of unconventional solutions to solve the problem. Broadcast this message unconventionally, and possibly without using words.

Consider things that your audience members regularly pass by each day but without giving them much thought. Take these things, and use them to do something out of the ordinary.

Guerrilla marketing has now gone digital. Therefore, think about all the places that your target audience is especially online. They could be on various social media sites such as Facebook, Twitter, Instagram, and other sites. Think about creative ambush ads and give them a show they will always remember. While you shouldn't encourage lying, you should be creative and come up with eye-popping and possibly even shocking but positive guerrilla marketing ads.

Chapter 5: Popular Social Media Marketing Sites

As a business owner seeking to grow your business, attract more customers, promote your brand and generally be profitable, you will need to come up with an appropriate marketing strategy that will work for your business. One of the most effective ways of doing this is to go multichannel. This means using different channels to promote the business, market the products, and advertise the brand.

Social media marketing has become the most crucial platform for all businesses both large and small. Digital marketing has focused a lot more on social media and it is a trend that no business owner can afford to miss out on. Social media marketing is about building unique relationships and engaging with online users because they have the potential of becoming your customers one day.

Why choose social media marketing?

A lot of business owners still do not understand why they need to use social media. They still haven't understood the reach and power of these social networking websites. A lot of them still think that social media sites are a waste of time where users gossip and spend time doing non-productive activities. Some business owners even prohibit their employees or workers from accessing social networking sites at work.

The failure of all these people to understand and fathom the power of social media is causing them to lose out on the numerous advantages that these platforms have to offer. They should copy and follow what numerous other business owners are doing. A lot of enterprising individuals and firm owners have come to understand and appreciate the power of social media.

Two basic ways of using social media

There are two main methods of using social networking sites as part of your marketing strategy. These include word-of-mouth, advice and all recommendations from friends and family. This kind of confidence will boost your business and promote your brand. This particular piece of advice holds true both online and offline. Social media sites have now become the online equivalent of traditional word-of-mouth marketing technique.

With social media, you are able to read, comment, share and generally interact with others when a message is posted. This is a powerful way of getting a message out to consumers. Business owners are able to make use of social media to implement their digital marketing campaigns. All that they need to do is to create the relevant content and then share it on social media. Others will pick it up from there.

However, the content will need to add value to the lives of social media users. They need to see some value in the content that you post as a business owner. Therefore, take your time to think about appropriate content that your viewers would love to see. To do this effectively, you will have to understand them and know what their main problems, issues, and challenges are. Once you have an understanding of their issues and challenges, you will be able to create quality content that is interesting to read or watch, fun, and adds value.

There is another way of using social networking websites for marketing a small business online. This is through the use of paid advertising. A lot of all the major social media sites provide ways for businesses to advertise their merchandise. The advertising can attract a huge following and with far-reaching effects at very affordable rates. Many users of social networks receive advertising messages every once in a while. A lot of them follow the messages if they are well presented.

As a business owner, you need to understand and learn how to combine these two techniques in order to promote your business, enhance your brand, and increase your sales. These two strategies, when combined properly, can propel your business to great heights and provide you with the kind of success that you could only dream about.

Advantages of Social Media Advertising

There are numerous advantages of advertising on social media. One of these benefits is direct interaction with customers. It is not easy for businesses to get into contact with customers. This would normally cost a lot of money and small businesses do not have this kind of money.

However, through social media websites, business owners can reach an extremely large base of potential customers as well as general social media users and followers. Interacting with customers gives you a chance to learn about their wants and needs, what works and what doesn't as well as generally learn about who they are and where they live.

You are able to reach out to a broader or wider audience than what is possible through traditional marketing methods. Social media sites such as Facebook, Twitter, and Instagram have followers in the billions or hundreds of millions in most cases. Gaining access to such a large pool of users propels you to an advantageous position.

You also get to reach out to a targeted audience. While it is common to advertise to a wide audience using traditional marketing methods, social media allows you to market your business and brand to a smaller and more localized audience. This targeted audience is probably one that has a direct interest in your products and the services that you provide.

Instagram for Business

Create an appealing and creative Instagram profile

Instagram is a globally popular social networking website. It is well known as the best site for sharing photos, videos, and images of all kinds. If you have a tangible product that you are selling, then beautiful photos that are large, clear, and colorful will fair very well on this platform. Business owners need to have an Instagram page which can be used to interact with members and share images and videos in order to promote their brands and businesses.

Instagram has over 800 million users each day who spend roughly thirty minutes browsing through images and videos on the platform. Such a huge daily audience presents plenty of opportunity for your business and brand. However, you first need to create an appealing business page.

To do this, you will need to be very creative. Remember there are plenty of other businesses within your niche. As such, you need to bring you're A-game to the table. This means creating a professional website that contains your business name and clearly displays your brand name.

Include your business address, official name, online address such as your URL, and ensure that you are consistent with the images, brand, and business name. Instagram allows you to provide sufficient contact and business information.

You should follow this by providing absolutely clear and beautiful images that are captivating and memorable. Tell a story with each image and allow your audience to enjoy the images, share your posts and interact in any other way.

Increase your Instagram reach using these simple tricks

There are many reasons why Instagram account holders need a large following. If you want to increase your reach, then you will need to increase the visibility of your posts. Reach simply refers to the people who get to view your posts. When more people get to view your posts, you will get more followers and hopefully more customers. Here are some tips on how to skyrocket your reach.

1. Ensure that you place your posts at the right time: The most important step in increasing your reach is having the right kind of post. Once you have the right, you should post it at the correct time. Timing is important because you want your audience to view the post. Find out when they are most active and available to check out their Instagram.

2. Have your primary goal as engagements: If you want to increase your reach on Instagram, then you need to focus more on engagement. This should be your number one focus. First, create relevant and engaging content for your viewers. The content could be contests or giveaways. You could also ask some questions and basically engage your readers and followers. And remember to always include a call to action. For instance, you could say, "Tag a friend," "Follow this link," and so on.

And remember to keep the engagements in motion. Respond to queries, answer questions from your followers, share any content they share with you and generally engage them. Never ignore them otherwise you will not be able to hang on them for long.

3. Your hashtags should be optimized: Hashtags are important on major social media platforms such as Instagram. You need to make sure that you choose the right hashtags and then optimize them appropriately. Suitable hashtags are those that are related to your specific niche or industry. Posts with 11 or more hashtags tend to attract the highest engagements even though Instagram allows up to 30 hashtags per post. Always think about the marketing terms relevant to your niche. These are terms that your audience is probably searching for on social media. Use these terms on your posts and hashtags for a much wider reach.

4. Make use of video content: Video content on Instagram is said to attract a lot more attention compared to other content types. Users will engage much more on video than other posts. They are capable of generating double the engagements on other posts. You want your posts to attract more viewers and hence comments and likes will help to attract a lot more people to your page.

5. *Promote user-generated content:* You should recognize and acknowledge your followers. Sometimes you will find content from your followers. This content could be photos or videos for instance. First, curate this content and just focus on the most crucial parts. Once the content is ready, make sure to share it with your followers. An analysis of Instagram has shown that user-generated content greatly increases conversion rate. This rate increases, even more, when users interact with the shared post.

The Lifestyle / Business Model

There are generally two paths to follow when starting or running your own business. You could come up with a startup business or a lifestyle business. Startups are generally very involving and require huge amounts of capital. On the other hand, a lifestyle business is one where the owner is often the sole employee of the business and earns sufficient amounts to take care of his needs as well as the freedom to pretty much do whatever he or she wants.

A lot of startups fail. Generally, for every successful business such as Instagram, there are hundreds of others out there that failed miserably or barely surviving. You cannot afford to start a business whose chances of success are only 50% or less. This is why a lifestyle business model is more suitable for you compared to a startup.

Startups take up a lot of your time. You generally have to work from nine to five. While this can be exciting for a while, it can become exhausting. On the other hand, a lifestyle business allows you to work whenever you want and from any location around the world just as long as you have access to the internet.

Tools, apps, and software to increase your reach

If you want to increase your reach on Instagram, then you should do so using a number of tools and apps. There are more than 30 different tools, apps, and software that you can use to increase your reach. If you seriously want to enjoy huge growth and long-term success, then you should promote your brand and increase its visibility. Here are some tools and apps to help you along.

1. Viral Upgrade: This is basically a growth platform used by both influencers and brands. If you use this platform, you will be assigned an assistant who will help you to grow your account. The assistant will grow your account organically by engaging with your audience and growing your base. You will provide the desired demographics and the assistants will help with this.

2. Hoot Suite: It is important to post content regularly on your Instagram page. However, you are probably busy and cannot maintain a regular posting schedule. Fortunately, Hoot Suite can do exactly that for you. This is software designed to help with your scheduling. It will find suitable and appropriate content for your niche, caption the posts, and post on schedule.

3. Sprout Social: Success on social media platforms like Instagram is often gauged based on engagement. This means the number of likes, followers, comments and so on. This app enables you to view your engagements with followers as well as access to more useful data. For instance, you can find out the time when the most people view your posts and so on. You can also pre-schedule content posting and make the entire process faster, easier, and more organized.

4. Repost: Yet another useful software tool that you can use to increase your Instagram reach is Repost. This tool allows you to post images that you do not have a right to. It then gives credit to the poster. This way, you are able to post content or images from all over the web without flouting any copyright rules.

5. Social Insight: Sometimes it is difficult for brands to interact with each other and with followers due to time and size of followers. Fortunately, Social Insight allows businesses to manage and organize followers as well as scheduling posts at particular times. You can also receive analytics, so you learn what works and what does not.

Facebook

Facebook is the world's largest social networking website with more than 2 billion active users each month. As a small business owner and manager, you should have a presence on Facebook. This way, you will be able to use the opportunities available to reach out to this massive population. There are numerous marketing opportunities, brand promotion, and others that you can enjoy. You can have a Facebook business page, location page, or even be part of a group. Once you have a presence on Facebook and the page is live, you can then begin taking advantage of all the opportunities available.

Facebook groups

A Facebook group is a must-have for all local businesses. They are also essential for all other small businesses including those based online. Facebook recently made it possible for page owners to open groups relating to their own unique niches and feeds.

There are over 1 billion individuals that use Groups on Facebook. It is within the groups that like-minded users actually connect. This is why opening a group is important. Once you open a group page within Facebook, then you will attract hundreds of interested persons who are easier to engage with because of shared interests.

Facebook groups also provide analytics which will provide you with insights on how your group is performing and which tactics are working. Facebook groups come with group chats, built-in analytics, create polls and post documents, and notifications to members.

Skyrocketing your Facebook reach

There are certain things that you can do in order to enhance and increase your Facebook reach. It is your reach that will enable you to get more followers and expose your brand even further. Here are some ways you can do this.

1. Optimize content and then share it on Facebook

One of the things that you need to do on your Facebook page is to share content. When you share content, you engage your followers and possibly also their followers. Make sure that the content you share is outstanding, memorable, and evokes a reaction from viewers. Such content is likely to be shared by your followers. To reach an even wider audience, you should optimize your content. Optimizing means using hashtags and adding what is relative to your niche and industry.

2. Less is more so post less content

You need to try and post less content if you want to impact your viewers. Many times, Facebook users post a lot of content which sometimes overwhelms the audience who consider it spamming. Try and focus on very high-quality images or videos which are shared possibly once a day for a total of 4 days each week.

3. Engage your audience

You should always engage your audience, viewers, and followers. If they share any content, then make sure you engage. You can leave a comment, like, or share with your followers. If you post content and your viewers leave comments, make sure you respond to these comments. You could answer their questions, like their statements, and basically, engage them.

4. Target repeat visitors Facebook ads and emails

To reach out to more viewers and engage them even further, you should use indirect methods such as using ads and emails. Since you already have the right audience, it becomes very easy to reach out and promote your brand and advertise your products. Facebook has made it very easy for small businesses to engage their followers and reach out to a wider audience through groups and business pages.

5. Boost some of your best posts

You also need to focus on boosting some of your best posts. This is yet another way of reaching out to more viewers and increasing your reach. First, you should produce top-notch content. Any content that accumulates numerous engagements such as likes and shares can be promoted so that it reaches even more people across Facebook.

The Lifestyle – Business Model

There are different kinds of lifestyle businesses. However, most people think about a business where the founder pursues a passion and then forms a business around it. Like they say, "follow your passion and build a business around it." IF this approach is properly executed, then your business will thrive for years to come.

If you have a hobby, then you can build a business around it. In this case, instead of a blog, you should open a Facebook page. One of the challenges you can expect with this kind of business is traffic. Fortunately, Facebook has millions of users and account holders many of who share your interest. You stand a great chance of finding interested followers, fans, leads, and customers through Facebook.

This business approach is extremely beneficial compared to other businesses. Since you mostly do what you like, you get to enjoy every minute of it. And you do not have to work on your business on a full-time basis. You can choose your hours depending on when demand is high or when it gets busy.

Passion business is suitable for most people because there is no need for huge capital investments. You do not need a lot of money to get started like you would with other types of businesses such as a brick-and-mortar establishment or a startup.

Another benefit of this business approach is that you can manage it mostly from your social media pages. As a business person, you can take advantage of all the conveniences provided by social networking websites such as Facebook in order to get the word out, reach out to interested people, and get followers and customers.

Selling points of the lifestyle business approach

You get to grow as fast or as slow as you please. There is no pressure, no shareholders, and no urgency at all but only what you want. A lifestyle business is designed to provide you with a comfortable lifestyle. It is up to you to define the comfort you desire.

You do not have to fall sick working for someone else. A lot of people put on weight because they have to sit for long hours working at someone else's business. If you want to head to the gym or prepare a meal in the afternoon, you are at liberty to do so.

You do not have to be tech-savvy to start your own business. You can start your own business and manage it well without having to come up with a technical project. This approach is suitable for all people. However, research has shown that it favors women a lot more especially because of the challenges they experience at the traditional workplace. Think about all the challenges women have and then consider the kind of freedom that this business approach has to offer.

Tools, apps, and software to increase reach and ease things up

There are numerous tools available that you can use on Facebook to enhance your business activities. There are some excellent tools that you can use to help you to come up with custom Facebook pages and so much more. While most of them are free to use, there is a limitation when it comes to accessible features. Here are some tools that you can use.

1. Heyo: Heyo is a great tool that you can use on your Facebook business account. You can use it to create hashtag campaigns, contests, and sweepstakes. This tool will help to save you time as it provides free Facebook templates. You get creative control with the drag and drop editor. You also get to increase your reach via photo contests, sweepstakes, group deals and so much more.

2. Tab Site: Another interesting app that you can use with your Facebook page is Tab Site. This app enables you to create and then manage your very own custom Facebook pages. You also get to create and manage your Facebook apps and hold promotions. Tab Site also allows you to offer contents, deals, and multiple apps. The apps need no coding or programming and easy to use. You can use them for pixel perfect designs. You also able to do other things such as run video and photo contests, add product slideshows, add YouTube videos, import blog posts, run sweepstakes, and so much more.

3. Short Stack: The software Short Stack is a powerful tool used for app creation. It allows you, the user, to create powerful apps, campaigns, and landing pages without the need to learn anything new. Other things that you can do with this software program include unlimited campaigns, promotions, 5000 campaign visits per 30 days, export entries and leads, and so much more.

4. Woo Box: Woo Box is an app that helps Facebook users to run and manage campaigns on the platform. Numerous businesses use Woo Box for different purposes including the use of six different apps, to customize their Facebook tabs, HTML Fangate, photo contests, and so much more. This is an excellent tool to support all of your Facebook marketing, ad, and promotions.

5. Easy Tab Creator: This software is another that you can use with your Facebook business page. It features a pretty simple interface and can help you to manage up to three different pages absolutely free. This application runs on Facebook and enables you to customize your business page by adding all kinds of content including YouTube videos, text, and so on.

YouTube

YouTube is the second largest search engine and the largest video sharing platform on the internet. Users can share, post, and watch videos on YouTube for free. All you need to do is open an account which is easy if you already have a Gmail account. It is a very popular website with users from across America and all over the world.

Users visit the website to watch interesting, entertaining, and captivating videos, to learn through videos, and to obtain news and information. If you join YouTube, you will be able to post videos and share it with the hundreds of millions of users who log in every day to watch entertaining content. Most people who get onto YouTube do so to for information and entertaining. Take advantage of the 1.6 billion active monthly users to leverage and market your brand and business.

Skyrocket your YouTube traffic reach

1. Only post high-quality videos: If you want to be successful on YouTube and increase your reach, then you should focus on producing only high quality, exciting, memorable, and engaging videos. Make a point of learning how to produce good quality content which you can then share on your YouTube page for wider reach.

2. Make use of tools and apps to increase traffic: There are lots of tools provided by YouTube that you can use to increase your reach. For instance, you can use video editing tools and apps to improve the quality of your videos. This way, more people will view and share your content, increasing your reach.

3. Optimize your content: You are probably used to optimizing content for your blog or website. Now you need to learn to optimize content for YouTube as well. YouTube is a large search engine second only to Google. Therefore, optimize your videos so as to increase your reach.

4. Engage your viewers: All too often we tend to ignore our followers and those who comment on our videos. This is wrong and definitely not good for business. As a business owner seeking to increase your reach, you should engage your viewers, respond to their comments, and definitely encourage them to share the videos.

5. Post videos regularly: You need to post high quality, suitable edited and entertaining videos on a regular basis. Doing so will keep you relevant and will keep your viewers coming back for more. You will also enable them to share more of your content with their networks which is excellent as it increases your reach.

The lifestyle business model for YouTube

If you want to start your own stress-free business, then the best approach is to start a lifestyle business rather than any other. This kind of model allows you to create a business based on your passion.

Other business models such as brick-and-mortar may require you to remain open from 8.00 am to 5.00 pm, demand lots of hard work, and are possibly stressful. However, building a business around a hobby and passion allows you to work only as hard as you like and whenever you want. You can choose to work only mornings or only evenings then go to the gym or park and relax.

Businesses such as startups and others require large capital inputs and you have to search for investors or borrow loans. This will put you under a lot of pressure. Most startups never live beyond the first year, and the rest probably won't see the end of the fifth year.

If you start a lifestyle business, you can put it on social media platforms such as YouTube and find customers here. Your talent and passion will attract numerous like-minded people who will then become your followers and eventually your customers. You can expand exponentially through social media yet expend very little energy. It is advisable to focus on this business model compared to all others.

Tools, apps, and software to ease things and increase reach

Building a YouTube channel takes a lot of work especially if you are trying to grow your business. Fortunately, there are some amazing tools that you can use to help you with your channel. These tools and apps will help you to manage your channel, increase your reach, and edit your videos. Here are some of the tools and apps that you can use to enhance your YouTube channel.

1. Tube Buddy: Tube Buddy is considered the single most useful YouTube toolkit. It is an essential toolkit that you need to have if you are to be successful. It comes with more than 60 different features that help you with almost anything that you need. Tube Buddy will generally help you to promote your channel and videos, ensure that you are productive, and also aid with your YouTube SEO.

2. Snappa: If your YouTube channel is to grow and increase your reach, then you need a tool that lets you create excellent artwork and images. Snappa is among the top tools out there for YouTube videos. It will enhance your videos and enable you to come with great visuals through its premade templates. It is advisable to always use high-quality image editing and enhancing tools for your YouTube and Snappa is excellent even when compared to other tools in the market.

3. Creator Studio App: If you have a number of apps and wish to promote your business through them, then you will need some assistance. This is where the Creator Studio app comes in handy.

This is a powerful tool that lets you do just about everything on your YouTube channel except perhaps creating the original video. You also get to find out how your video is performing and receive metrics and lots of other things as well.

4. Wix: You will need this app if you plan to monetize your YouTube account. As a small business owner, your aim of using social media sites like YouTube is to help you find customers in order to sell your products for a profit. For this to happen successfully, you will need a website. There are plenty of website builders out there, but Wix is absolutely the best of them all. It is super easy to use and lets you design your website using amazing templates. You will not even need to learn coding.

5. Buffer: If you want to increase your reach, you will need to share your videos across different social media platforms. One of the best tools to share your videos is Buffer. This handy tool enables you to share your videos across different social media platforms. It helps you to schedule content posting on various social networks allowing you to save time while still maintaining a credible presence on these networks.

Twitter

As a social media platform, Twitter has grown to become a useful site and all businesses should consider having a presence here. Users get on Twitter to catch up with the latest news, share stores, videos, images, and so much more.
Now since almost all businesses and users are on Twitter, it is easy to get lost unless you make an effort to stand out. This is the only way to stand out on Twitter. Here is how you can skyrocket your reach on Twitter.

1. Get to know your audience: There are hundreds of millions of users who check out Twitter each day. Not all these Twitter users are your audience though. You want your tweets and all other posts to be viewed by the right people who are your target audience.

Therefore, find people interested in your niche, those discussing industry matters and those searching for your products. If you are able to identify your audience, then you will get off to a great start.

2. Make use relevant hashtags: If you want to reach more people, especially those relevant to your industry, then you need to use hashtags that relate to your niche. Most people on Twitter use hashtags regularly as they bundle people together. Whenever you produce content, try and include a couple of hashtags. Keep them short and never use more than three at a time.

3. Engage your audience and talk with them: Your audience will comment on your posts, share, ask questions, and generally engage with your brand. As a business owner, you should talk to your audience and followers. Respond to their comments, answer their questions, share their posts and generally make sure that you engage in a positive manner, so they feel worthy and appreciated.

4. Find the best times to tweet and post content: Twitter is among other time-sensitive platforms. You need to know when to post your content. It has been noted that the best time to tweet is 5.00 pm for highest retweets and between 12.00 noon and 6.00 pm to have the highest reach. However, this does not work the same way for all brands. Fortunately, there are apps such as Follower Wonk and Audiense that can help you to figure out the best ad posting times.

5. Post content regularly: Content on Twitter has a very brief lifespan. Something posted in the morning may become obsolete before lunchtime. This is common on Twitter rather than other social networks. Therefore, post content about 4 times per day about 5 days each week. This way, you will help your brand to remain relevant.

How to sell the lifestyle-business model

One of the best ways to start a successful online business is to pursue the lifestyle business model. This model is renowned because it is centered on your hobby and passion. As such, you are not under serious pressure for any reason and can choose when to work and how much to work.

A business that is focused around your passion does not need to cost a lot of money to establish and set up. Most of your work can be done online and only when you want to. For instance, you will not need to spend money or incur expenses finding customers. All your customers can be sourced from social media sites. Twitter is an excellent platform that you can use to establish your business and reach out to potential customers. You will find plenty of customers via social media especially if you use the right hashtags and focus on individuals interested in your niche. The lifestyle business will not stress you out unnecessarily as there is no rent to pay, no loans to service and no bosses to answer to.

Tools and software to ease things for you and increase reach

Twitter is a fantastic platform for business. If you wish to grow your business and find new followers and customers, then you need to be on this platform. However, this might prove to be a challenge because most other businesses in your industry are also here.

Fortunately, with the use of tools, you can make things easier for you. There are tools that help with curating and sharing content, scheduling posting, increasing reach and so much more. Here is a look at some tools that will help you get ahead.

1. Hoot Suite: One of the best and most versatile tools that you need for your Twitter account is Hoot Suite. This tool is fantastic at getting you organized. You can post all your tweets as well as photos and videos via this amazing tool. Hoot Suite can help you schedule posting so that you prepare content which is then posted at a more appropriate time. You also get to keep a track of what is happening on your account.

2. Buffer: Automatic posting is something you need to consider especially if you are a heavy Twitter user. As a business owner, you are probably quite busy and need help with your social media accounts. Buffer is the tool that you need to accomplish this task. It can post content on your behalf across multiple social platforms and allow you to attend to other matters.

3. Twitter Counter: Yet another tool available to Twitter users is Twitter Counter. This tool provides graphs and basic analytics about tweets and followers. You can learn about the statistics and figures for each day, week, and month. The tool also creates content automatically and produces statistics in real time.

4. Social Oomph: This is a tool that provides you with lots of services that you need. Services include auto following anyone who follows you on Twitter. The app allows you to create automated messages which are sent as replies to your followers. It also enables you to schedule future tweets, so you do not have to worry about your social media when you are attending to other duties.

5. Tweet Adder: One of the best tools out there for adding Twitter followers to your account very fast is Twitter Adder. This particular tool easily adds about 150 followers in your niche each day. These are real followers who are within your industry and are genuinely interested in your niche. When followers are added to your account, this tool sends them an automated thank you message and also does replies.

Pinterest

Social media has changed the way we do business. We are now able to create communities and direct traffic to our websites and at the same time develop lasting relationships. One platform that is capable of all these is Pinterest. This platform that is, however, not utilized as much as it should. Yet it can direct plenty of traffic your way and increase your reach.

1. Create Pinterest pins that direct to valuable sites: Pinterest now focuses on displaying pins leading to valuable resources and blog posts. You may have a beautiful image, but if it does not lead to any useful resources, then it will not be prominently displayed. Therefore, come up with a useful website or blog and ensure your pins redirect there.

2. Grow both your reach and followers: While it is important to gain as many followers as possible, you should focus more on creating pins that are likely to reach people not using Pinterest. For instance, think about pins so great that your followers will share with others so that they go viral. This way, you stand a chance of going viral and possibly reaching millions of people.

3. Make use of keywords on board names: Your boards will appear on interest feeds and in the "Picked for You" list if there is a relevant and suitable title. For instance, if you are targeting tourists, then your board can have a title like Travel Tips.

4. A number of keywords should be used: Pinterest mostly resembles a search engine where millions of individuals carry out searches looking for ideas, for gifts, and all manner of things. Your brand and businesses are more likely to be found by these millions of potential customers when you use the correct keywords. Therefore, always think beyond your current followers, use relevant keywords, and reach out even to people, not on Pinterest.

5. Join a Group Board: You need to consider joining board groups in order to increase your reach. Many business owners and individuals join group boards in order to have pins exposed to as many people as possible. Take time to identify relevant group boards. This way, your pins will be exposed to hundreds of thousands of people within the same group.

The lifestyle-business model

There are numerous different business ideas that you can choose. However, some require a lot of capital while others demand a lot of your time and attention. If you do not have a lot of time or attention, then you probably want to start a lifestyle business. A lifestyle business is generally created out of a hobby or passion that you have. Such a business is highly likely to be successful because you probably understand everything about it, have passion and enjoy doing things related to it. You do not need a lot of resources to get started. You are free to start small and grow at your own pace.

Therefore, you do not need to borrow money from family and friends to get started. You also do not need to seek investor funding as most startups do. Many startups fail within the first year and most others will not get to their third birthday. However, most lifestyle businesses succeed because of the simplicity of the business as well as the passion of the business owner and freedoms that it has to offer.

Remember that a successful business is one that affords you freedom, one where you determine the pace, and one where you have a healthy balance between work and relaxation only a lifestyle business can afford you this kind of success even in the long term.

Tools and apps to increase reach and ease things for you

Pinterest is fast becoming among the most trusted and best apps that people use when they need information. Putting your business on this platform is a major plus. However, you need to work a little harder if you want to beat the competition and succeed. If you are managing multiple channels, then you will need some help with your social media accounts. Fortunately, that help is readily available through tools, software, and apps. Here are some tools that can help you achieve success on Pinterest.

1. Buffer: Buffer is a tool that helps you find great pins from different websites which are then added instantly to your Pinterest account. Also, you could be browsing across Pinterest and notice something that catches your eye. You could easily pin this to your social media accounts using a tool provided on Buffer. Another useful feature is that you have access to stats showing how your pins are performing. These include likes, re-pins, and comments.

2. Tailwind: This is a great tool for your Pinterest account and can help you manage almost all activities. It also comes with some interesting analytics, so you get the statistical information that you need. Therefore, you are able to schedule posts, receive important statistics and also get to analyze the competition and see the activity of your influential followers.

3. ViralWoot: ViralWoot is a useful Pinterest tool that offers a number of exciting features. These include a tool for growing your followers, one for scheduling, another for pin alerts, and one for placing advertisements. However, it is not free and there is a monthly fee to pay.

4. Loop88: This is a tool designed to specifically help you to increase reach and gain more followers. Loop88 is a Pinterest tool that connects your account to important influencers within your industry. The influencers, especially those with engaged followers are connected with brands and advertisers. You will enjoy lots of re-pins, exposure, and numerous additional followers.

5. Pinterest widgets: This consists of a free list of tools that you can use in order to integrate your website with your Pinterest account. There are about five separate widgets. The first is the pin it button which enables you to pin images from your website. Then there is the follow button which makes it easy for people to follow you on Pinterest directly from your website. Others are the profile, board, and pin widgets all of which play a crucial role in integrating your site and Pinterest account.

LinkedIn

The social website LinkedIn is thought of as the Facebook or social media for business. A lot of business executives and professionals do not see much need for platforms such as Facebook and Instagram find a welcoming home on LinkedIn. This is because LinkedIn connects them with businesses, business leaders, other professionals, and work-related opportunities. If you have a LinkedIn account, there are ways that you can increase your reach and promote your presence. Here are some of these ways

Skyrocket your reach on LinkedIn

1. Start by optimizing your page: LinkedIn generally wants its members to have complete profiles so that it's easy for others to track them down and recognize them. It also makes it easy to access opportunities and connect with others. For instance, you should provide all your official names, an address, and contact information. Also, make use of relevant keywords within your industry. A complete profile is a great way to increase your reach on LinkedIn.

2. Get active and remain that way: Having a LinkedIn account is not enough. You need to become active and use the account often. You can choose to follow others, invite others to follow you, read the blogs, and engage your followers. Other things you can do include joining groups, updating your status, and letting others know what you are up to.

3. Recommend and endorse others: While you want others to endorse and recommend you, you need to be doing the same on LinkedIn. When you recommend others, you will stand out as an authority figure and earn the respect of your peers. You will also increase your activity on the platform which will, in turn, enhance your reach.

4. Invite people from your official email address: An easy way of getting more followers is to search for people you already know on LinkedIn and inviting those that are not members. LinkedIn has a feature that helps you to achieve this quite easily.

5. Post and share content: If you want to increase your reach on LinkedIn, then you need to come up with great content and share it on the platform. The content can be a blog or article or any other relevant type. Ensure that the information provided is beneficial to professionals on the platform and make sure you use relevant keywords.

The Lifestyle Business

If you have a lifestyle that you are used to, then you can always make a business out of it. A lifestyle business can be started so as to help fund your lifestyle. Your business can be online, but the main aim will be to promote your lifestyle and benefit financially from it.

Such businesses are typically started with little or no financial resources. There are also no shareholders, no external partners, no bank loans and no venture capital. This leaves the owner with a lot of control over the business. The owner can also choose how fast or slow they want the business to grow.

Lifestyle businesses generally last many years especially compared to other types of businesses. These include an e-commerce store, a bed and breakfast, consultancy services, and blogging or writing. One of the benefits that you will enjoy operating a lifestyle business is the freedom of time. You will be free to choose when to work and when to do whatever you desire.

You also get to enjoy the choice of location. There are no requirements regarding the location and as the boss, you get to operate your lifestyle business from any location that you like. Another benefit that you stand to enjoy is financial freedom. You have the freedom to determine how large or fast you want your business to grow. In return, you get to determine your paycheck as well as income.

Tools, apps, software to manage and increase your reach on Linked

LinkedIn has become *the* social networking website for business executives, professionals, and business owners. It has also become a central hub for business to business selling. Recent statistics indicate that LinkedIn now has over 500 million members and over 80% of B2B selling originates here. To be successful on this social networking website, you need to increase your reach and manage the account appropriately. Here are some tools that can help enhance this.

1. Resume builder: LinkedIn has created a resume builder which you can use to turn your resume on the platform into an MS Word or PDF document. The process of doing so is very easy and fast and anyone can do it. Once you convert your LinkedIn resume into a PDF or MS Word document, you can then share it via Twitter, Facebook, LinkedIn, or to anyone on your email address. You can also edit, rearrange, print, and export details on the resume using the resume builder.

2. Rapportive: This app has been around for a couple of years and is great at supercharging your LinkedIn profile. It remains as effective today as it has always been. This tool is actually an extension of Chrome web browser and connects seamlessly with your Gmail account. Should you receive an email from a LinkedIn member, their profile will instantly appear in form of a summary so that you get a clear indication about the sender.

3. E-Link Pro: If you are looking to sell via LinkedIn, then one of the tools that you need to use is E-Link Pro. You first need to install this tool via your Chrome browser as an extension. Then you will develop a search queue of your target customers so they can be searched on LinkedIn. Once ready, just click on "Play" and E-Link Pro will begin the search. It will go through 800 different profiles searching for your target buyers. Most of these contacts will notice that you viewed their profiles. They will probably check you out and express an interest in what you are offering.

4. Hunter: This is an excellent tool that helps you locate the email address of anyone that you want. If you visit a profile and wish to find the email address of that member, then Hunter will track down the member's email and avail it.

5. Infinity: Infinity is a visualization tool for LinkedIn. It is used to showcase your professional network designed and built using Javascript APIs. All you need to do to get started is to log in by choosing "Sign in with LinkedIn." Once logged in, you can click then drag in order to zoom in and out, navigate through your contacts, and also search by status update, title, and name.

10 Mistakes People Make when Marketing on Social Media

By now, most business owners understand the need to advertise and market their businesses on social media. They have opened pages and accounts across different social media sites especially the major ones such as Facebook and Twitter. However, having a presence only is not sufficient. People still make mistakes on these social sites which cost them followers, leads, opportunities, and potential customers. Here are some mistakes that people make when marketing on social media.

1. Not posting regularly

There are people who open social media accounts and then forget about them. They probably think that having a presence on popular social media sites like Instagram and Facebook is enough. This is wrong and you will not attract any followers or customers. As a business owner, you should post content on a regular basis. Basically, you should post 4 or 5 times per week on Facebook and about 4 times per day for five days per week on Twitter.

2. Being on only one channel

Some people open an account or page on only one social media. They consider only that particular platform as important and the rest insignificant. This is wrong because you stand a better chance of success on multiple social media sites. Marketing across multiple social media sites is absolutely crucial for the success of your brand and business.

3. Dismissing social media marketing as ineffective:

Some people believe that social media is not suitable for their niche or industry. This is a common misconception where people believe that social media marketing is either for young people and millennials or for tech-savvy individuals. This is not true as the fastest growing demographic is people aged 45 to 54 on Facebook and those aged 55 to 65 years on Twitter. All other demographics are well represented too. Social media is very effective when it comes to marketing. Companies and businesses not using social media are losing out big time on the opportunities presented here.

4. Ignoring your followers

On many occasions, business owners with social media pages tend to ignore their followers. They think responding to comments or engaging in any other way with them is a waste of time. However, this is a grave mistake that will make your social media marketing efforts flounder. You followers may like your posts and content. If so they will leave comments, ask questions, and share your content with others. You need to get online and engage them. This is the best way to grow your account and gain new followers. Failure to do this will see your followers ignore your page and leave to follow your competitors.

5. Not dealing appropriately with negative social media feedback

All businesses fear negative feedback on social media. However, when this happens, an appropriate response is necessary. Such comments should not be ignored. Instead, any issues raised should be addressed, any necessary remedies should be offered, and an appropriate solution sought. Negative criticism should be viewed as an opportunity to improve and get things right. The person who left the comments should be politely approached and their specific issue addressed publicly if necessary so that all followers and audience see you actually taking action to remedy the situation.

6. Spamming

As much as it is important to post content and share with others, this should be done strategically and in moderation. Some people will use multiple links, numerous hashtags, and marketing messages with their content. Others keep reposting old posts and so on. This kind of spammy behavior is unacceptable and will annoy your followers.

7. Overly promoting yourself

Social networking websites are best for sharing, socializing, and communicating. Even as you have a marketing strategy and wish to promote your products and brand, you need to do so in moderation. Social media users have become averse to adverts and detest marketing and promotional content. They prefer to engage normally with brands. If you have to promote your business and brand, then do so subtly and tactfully.

8. Unreal followers

There are business owners who pay to have followers. However, paid followers are often not real followers. They may not be interested in your brand or industry. You will make very little headway with fake or unreal followers. Make sure that you grow your followers organically and within your industry. This way, you will receive followers that are genuinely interested in your products and your brand.

9. Posting poor quality content

As a business owner, you should post high-quality content that adds value to your followers' lives. All too often people will post average, low-quality posts that add little value to the lives of their social media followers. They will quickly start to ignore your page and posts altogether. This will be a disaster. You need to take time to come up with high-quality content that is memorable, intriguing, funny, and probably worth sharing.

10. Not having a well-thought-out plan

Before getting onto social media and opening a page for your business, you must think about your desires, ambitions, and goals. Take time and think about what you wish to achieve through your social media pages. Have a well-defined strategy and create a good plan. The plan should outline your budget, goals, and key performance indicators (KPI). This way, you will be able to achieve a lot more.

Chapter 6: Paid Advertising – Getting Paid Traffic

Businesses need to focus on marketing and advertising if they are to achieve growth, expansion, sales, and profits. The success of your business will largely be pegged on your marketing strategies and advertising is a major part of marketing. You should take time and come up with a successful marketing strategy that will see you achieve your ambitions.

What is paid advertising?

Paid advertising simply refers to advertising services that you have to pay for as compared to other forms such as earned advertising. Earned advertising may include word-of-mouth which you do not have to pay for.

Online advertising involves a lot of earned advertising. If you want success, sometimes you have to pay for it. There are different types of paid advertising. These include the following;

- Video ads
- Pay per click
- Pay per download
- Display ads
- Pay per view

Why are ads important?

One of the reasons why you should use advertising is that you get instant results. If you set up an ad, then you are likely to start receiving responses almost immediately. You will also start receiving increased traffic to your social media pages as well as your website. It is also an affordable yet effective way of bringing customers to your store.

The best place to start your advertising is on your chosen social media. Since Facebook is the largest social networking website with billions of followers. For this reason, it is advisable to begin your paid ads campaign here. You can then move to YouTube, Instagram, and Twitter. These four are among the best social media sites to begin your paid ads campaigns.

Ad Copies: An ad copy is the main text of a click advert. The ad copy has a number of elements including credibility, attention, the promise of a benefit, as well as a call to action.

Advertising also helps to keep your brand relevant. By regularly advertising, you will remain relevant in the eyes of your customers and social media followers.

Facebook

Facebook Ads have a micro-targeting feature. This feature allows you to reach the audience that you desire based on factors such as interests, location, and demographics.

Types of Facebook ads

- Photos ads
- Video ads
- Carousel ads
- Slideshow ads
- Instant ads

Cost of Facebook ads: The cost of Facebook ads varies depending on several factors. Daily amounts can be charged which will hardly exceed $11. If you choose to run your ad continuously, then expect to pay no more than $77 each week.

Instagram

Instagram ads are very similar to Facebook ads. There is no set amount for advertising and advertisers get to choose their own budgets. This gives you leeway to choose your preferred approach.

Cost of Instagram advertising: You should expect to pay anywhere from $0.20 to $2 for CPC or cost per click ads. You can opt for cost per mile ads which cost about $5 per 100 visitors.

Analytics: Instagram provides you with analytics. Focus only on merits that you can change. You should use the information obtained to improve your marketing.

Types of ads

- 30-second video ads
- Instagram marquee
- Multi-photo carousel ads
- Picture ads
- Interactive navigation

YouTube

YouTube ads are different from all others because YouTube is primarily a video sharing platform. There are several types of YouTube ads. These include;

- Display ads
- Bumper ads
- Skippable ads
- Non-skippable ads

Cost of YouTube ads: The cost of YouTube ads ranges from $0.10 to $0.30 for CPV or cost per view. You will pay $20 for your ad to reach 100,000 viewers.

Analytics: YouTube provides analytics for your videos. The analytics feature watch time reports, revenue reports, and interaction reports. You will want to focus on watch time views, the number of views, traffic sources, demographics, audience retention, and devices used to view your ads.

Twitter

Advertising on Twitter helps businesses to reach out to their followers, potential customers, and a target demographic. There are a number of different Twitter ads. These are;

- App card
- Lead generation card
- Photo card
- Gallery card
- Website card
- Player card

We also have;

- Promoted trends
- Promoted accounts
- Promoted tweets

Cost of Twitter Ads: The cost of a promoted tweet is $1.35 per engagement. Promoting a Twitter account costs between $2.50 and $4 per follower.

Twitter analytics: You should use analytics to find out the performance of your account and ads. There are some crucial statistics that you should pay attention to. These include the effectiveness of your ads and so on.

5 Mistakes People make when Advertising

1. Overdoing the ads

Sometimes we tend to create too many ads. This can cost a lot of money and may be spammy. Instead of overdoing the ads, you should spend your money on a few high quality extremely effective ads. Think about superior artworks and hire experts to help you prepare your ads.

2. Assuming that a business owner knows best

Sometimes we think that the business owner knows everything about the business, brands, and products. While this may be true, it is sometimes best to bring in an expert or outsider to prepare the advertisement. This way, you will get an objective view about the product and the right questions will be answered by the ad.

3. Making unsubstantiated claims

Advertisers sometimes make claims that they cannot substantiate. They often tend to say what customers want to hear and promising to solve all their problems. However, the product or brand may not be able to do everything claimed by the advertised. It is crucial to stick to the truth and not to make unsubstantiated claims.

4. Poor timing

It so often happens that advertisers place their ads at the wrong time. This happens especially when they place ads on Thursdays and Fridays just before people go shopping. This results in too many ads posted on these two days and the competition becomes extremely high. Placing ads on other days of the week could be just as effective but with less competition.

5. Targeting everyone

Advertisers fail when they try to target the entire market with their ads. They forget that niche markets are a lot more effective. It takes a lot more work and resources to post ads to the entire marketing.

Targeted marketing within a niche or industry is a lot more effective yet costs less.

Conclusion

Social media marketing and advertising are essential for the success of small businesses. Numerous businesses have grown and thrived simply by capitalizing on opportunities found on social networking sites.

Major social networks such as Facebook, Twitter, Instagram, YouTube, Pinterest, and LinkedIn provide numerous opportunities to businesses of all sizes. This is because they have large numbers of users and most of these users are also consumers. Most consumers love to spend time on social media posting photos and socializing with their friends and families.

If you own a small business and wish to market your brand on social media, then you need to first determine which ones are the most relevant for your business. First, identify your customers and determine which social networks they are likely to be on.

Once you identify the right social networks, you should craft quality advertisements messages targeted at your specific industry. If you do this correctly, then you will benefit from the numerous opportunities offered by social networking websites. You will grow your following and increase your reach, acquire more customers, increase your sales, and also earn more profits.

If you found the first part of this book helpful, please leave a positive review on Amazon as it allows me to keep producing quality books.

Personal & Business Branding

Go Viral And Make Unlimited Passive Income Building A Loyal Brand Network Through Blogging, SEO, Instagram, Facebook Advertising, YouTube, Email And Affiliate Marketing

Joshua Reach

Introduction

The Online Entrepreneurial Lifestyle

We can define entrepreneurship as the will and ability to start, run, manage, and organize a new business complete with all its challenges and risks in order to be profitable and earn money out of it. It is said that the most successful entrepreneurs are those that persevere through good and bad times.

An internet or online entrepreneur is an entrepreneur, manager, founder, or owner of a business that is largely or solely based on the internet. Such an entrepreneur earns their money through initiative and by taking certain calculated risks.

Why Start an Internet-Based Business?

There are benefits of starting an online business compared to other businesses that are especially brick-and-mortar-based. You can operate just about any business-type online. This means that you are not limited to small-time gigs such as selling your second-hand items. Some of the largest firms in the world are web-based. They include Amazon, Google, and Facebook.

Online businesses allow you to pursue your dreams and follow your passion. The nature of online business allows you to pursue your passion. This is in contrast to employment where you implement the company's vision and make someone else rich.

Having your own internet based business expands your earning potential. The challenge of working for someone else as an employee is that your earnings are limited to your salary. You will hardly have time to put in extra hours at another job or business. But, as a self-employed individual, you will be able to earn as much as you like depending on your hard work and business model.

You get to choose the hours that you work. The freedom to choose your own working hours means that you can choose to start work early or mid-morning, in the afternoon, or evening and work for as long as you want. This is because the internet is readily available and open for business all the time every single day. Having this kind of freedom is extremely liberating and will improve your quality of life immensely.

You will also save money on costs such as rent and overheads. Ordinary businesses such as brick-and-mortar stores and establishments have to pay a lot of money for rent, overheads, and costs such as salary and so on. On the contrary, most of these costs are eliminated if you work online. You do not need to pay any rent if you work from home. You will also not need employees as you can hire online at much cheaper rates should the need arise.

Build a Loyal Brand and Earn Millions for Many Years to Come

As an online business owner, you need to pay attention to building a strong, loyal brand. Online customers browse the internet in search of products they wish to buy before actually making the purchase. As such, you need to learn the modern ways of building brand loyalty. Here are some tips on how to go about it.

1. Engage your customers

When you connect with your followers, you introduce a feeling of belonging. You should endeavor to share any new developments and exciting news about your brand with your followers. You should also share your opinions so that they are excited and remain engaged. Some of the best platforms to use include popular social networks such as Facebook and Instagram.

2. Be authentic

If you want your customers and followers to trust you and remain loyal, then you should be authentic. This means showing your true self and staying true to your beliefs. Customers will detect anything phony or fake. This will work against you. However, being genuine, honest, decent, and authentic will result in long term trust and customer loyalty.

3. Remain consistent always

After working so hard to define your brand and connect with customers, you will need to remain consistent in what you do. Customers love consistency once they find what they want. Therefore, always refer back to what produced the success and drew customers to your brand. For instance, your messages and logo should be consistent at all times with little or no variation. Also, take the chance to share your values with your audience as often as possible.

4. Understand what makes your customers happy

A lot of businesses fail and brands fare poorly simply because they do not take the time to understand what the customers really want. Customers often abandon a brand when what is offered is different from what they want. Therefore, keep engaging your customers and provide them with opportunities to share their thoughts and opinions. Some businesses offer products that have no space in the market. It is always a great idea to listen to your customers and understand what they want then give it to them.

5. Invest in a professional-looking logo design

If you want brand loyalty, then you should always start with a professional looking logo. This way, if you have good quality products and a powerful brand, then your customers will always identify your brand through your logo. Take time to choose the design and colors carefully so that it exhibits your mood, feeling, and the role that your brand intends to fulfill.

Platforms to Promote Your Brand

There are a number of platforms that you need to use in order to promote your brand successfully. These include the largest social media platforms available today. They include Facebook, Twitter, YouTube, LinkedIn, Pinterest, and Instagram.

We know that almost 80% of adults in the US have social media accounts. Chances are that your customers are also on social media. Promoting your brand on these platforms is, therefore, an excellent way of reaching out to your customers and finding followers who can be converted into customers.

Even as you open accounts and pages for your brand, you should find ways of marketing your personal brand to followers. You should use both paid advertisements as well as options such as word of mouth and organic searches.

Your Personal Brand

If you want to impact your customers and the market greatly, then you need to develop a powerful personal brand. Such a brand connects easily connects a face to a brand or company. This is crucial if customers and the general public are to relate you to your brand.

A powerful personal brand can help you to develop a million-dollar business earning you millions each year easily. You can even develop your personal brand and become a thought leader. This way, people will follow you, buy your books and videos and pay to listen to you speak.

Start from nothing to something

Building your own business does not require much. All that you need in order to get started are a good business idea that addresses a particular problem and passion, energy, and zeal. If you have a burning desire to succeed and your idea solves a specific problem, then you will be on your way to building a successful enterprise.

If you have a hobby, talent or skill, then focus on it and develop it so that it is profitable in the long run. For instance, if you are a great designer with programming skills, then you can create beautiful web content for numerous clients over the internet.

E-commerce and leveraging the internet

If you want to succeed in business today, then you need to learn how to leverage the internet. You should endeavor to learn as much as you can about online entrepreneurship so that you can take advantage of this platform, grow your personal brand, and make huge profits with a great strategy. There are a couple of things you will need to know in order to succeed in your online ventures.

Perseverance

According to some of the most successful online entrepreneurs, the difference between successful online entrepreneurs and failures is perseverance. While it is sometimes tempting and easy to throw in the towel, it is absolutely important that you learn to persevere even when times are hard. Steve Jobs, the founder of Apple Inc., one of the largest and most successful computer companies in the world, once said that the most important trait of a successful business owner is perseverance.

Come up with a suitable business model

You should build a good business model that you can follow and adhere to as you grow and prosper. Such a plan is very similar to a pre-planned flight path that a plane takes in order to arrive at its destination safely. Basically, if there is no business model, then your business may not grow towards success as desired. This is akin to a plane not following a flight path. Such a plane will not arrive at its destination.

Once you establish your business, you should allow it to grow. This means putting in the hard work to build your brand, come up with a marketing plan and implement it across multiple channels. Experience has shown that it is crucial that you allow your business to grow. This means being flexible and letting your chosen business model evolve and expand. This is common especially in today's world of internet-based entrepreneurship.

Your customers will, with time, desire change and a different direction. If your business directs you that way, then you should be willing to make adjustments and accept the changes. In essence, it is crucial to put the interests of your customers first and make any necessary changes in order to remain relevant.

Chapter 1: The Mindset of a Determined Entrepreneur

As an entrepreneur, you probably dream of success and quitting your day job. Maybe you want to earn millions of dollars and live a great life. Statistics show that over 85% of all employees worldwide desire to be doing something else rather than their current jobs.

Even then, quitting your job and setting up a business is just the beginning because there is a lot of work that needs to get done. To establish yourself and your personal brand, you need to put in a lot of long hours and hard work. The first step though should be spent on learning about how to become an entrepreneur. Learning entrepreneurship is often underrated but is the best thing that you can do for yourself if you are to emerge the winner.

Have a Plan and the Right Mindset

Some of the things you will need to do in order to get started include your finances, having a plan, goals, and a well-prepared mind. Basically, your habits will dictate your success. If you maintain the 9 to 5 mindset, then you probably won't fare very well as an entrepreneur. You need to start thinking and acting like other top entrepreneurs who put in the hard work and spend many hours just working hard. In the initial stages, you will really need to work, work, and then work some more. Here are some tips on how to have the right mindset for success as a successful entrepreneur.

1. Train your mind to start thinking out of the box

Once you start your own business, the corporate mentality should exit the door. This means that your working hours will no longer be limited to 8 hours between 9.00 am and 5.00 pm. You will need to, at this stage, open your mind to new and exciting possibilities such as those that never existed as an employee.

If you have a vision and start doing things the unconventional way, people may begin to stop you. They may not understand your vision and desire for success. However, you should not let this stop you. You should be creative and come up with something different and new in order to be successful.

2. Develop both long-term and short-term visions

You should focus on developing a new kind of thinking that focuses on attaining a strategic goal. Basically, you need to have a vision for your brand and company. Have an idea about where you want your business to go and what path you will follow to get there. Being an entrepreneur, it is your vision that will guide your business even if you hire others to help you. The rest of your team will be looking up to you for leadership, guidance, and advice. You should be able to step up to the plate and provide the leadership needed.

3. Take charge and bear responsibility

Back when you were employed, you still got paid even when you had a bad day. In business, you might not get paid when your venture is unsuccessful. On top of not getting paid, there are others counting on you to get paid. While you may probably be able to manage without pay others cannot.

Starting a business sometimes causes an entrepreneur to experience high-stress levels. The stress can get so bad that it becomes a health issue. However, even under such severe stress, you still have to soldier on. You will need to learn to get over situations, muster the courage, and move on.

When you are working to establish your business and create your brand, you will need to motivate yourself. There will be no boss to encourage you and no supervisor around to see that you get the work done. For you to succeed, you will have to stay focused and organized and get used to plenty of hard work and long hours.

4. You will become a jack of all trades

Back when you were employed, you probably had a well-defined role to play. This time it will be different. As an entrepreneur, you will not be able to disown any job as there is no one else to pick up the slack. This will most certainly mean getting your hands dirty and doing work that you are not used to doing. Basically, you need to ensure that everything at your business is running along smoothly. You may need to do lots of tasks including accounting, customer service, IT work, and so much more.

Expect to learn different skills, do lots of menial tasks, and generally work long hours. You should not expect to have it easy at the initial stages. As an entrepreneur, you will not finish work when you get tired but when you are done.

5. Learn to be positive, focused, and flexible

In business, attitude is everything, so you need to always have the right attitude. You should never let any challenges get in the way of your vision. Always remember to be optimistic as every challenge that you meet has a solution. If you do not have the passion for entrepreneurship and building your brand, you may not get very far. As such, giving up is never going to be an option. Instead, have lots of passion in your work and focus on providing the best solution to a problem that a sector of the market has. Therefore, start off with a problem that needs to be solved or perhaps a great idea. Find a solution and do so with passion. This way, you will eventually be successful, and your brand will soar to great heights.

Mindsets that Will Make You a Successful Entrepreneur

One of the first things you need to get off your mind is the idea of getting rich very quickly. While times may be tough and opportunities hard to come by, there is always a chance to overcome the challenges and grow your business. Success and enterprise are often due to some changes and commitments that you make in your life.

Like most successful entrepreneurs, you want freedom in all aspects of your life. You also want to secure yourself and loved ones financially as well as leave them a secure future. You also have a sound product or solution that solves a problem or addresses a particular challenge that exists in society. Your solution should help make people's lives better.

If you can accomplish these feats, then you will become an unstoppable entrepreneur. All you will need to do is make some simple yet crucial adjustments to your life. If you can make these crucial adjustments to your life, then you can expect to see some results sooner or later. Here are a few tips that will help you along the journey.

Do not let expert assistance hold you down

Technology today allows us to receive training, coaching, and advice from anywhere around the world. Advances in technology allow for consultations to take place across vast distances. Therefore, you can consult an expert on a different continent or hire the services of a professional regardless of where they are located. Traveling long distances and spending a lot of money consulting is no longer necessary. These technological advances have provided immense help and opportunities for entrepreneurs, enabling them to take their businesses to the next level.

Even then you will need to be careful because after hiring a coach or consultant, you will start counting on him or her and develop a permission-seeking mindset which is unnecessary for an entrepreneur. There will be numerous times when you will need to make decisions and move forward regardless of all other factors. Therefore, learn to take advice from an expert where necessary but do not become too dependent on their advice. You should learn to be confident in your abilities and capacity to make sound decisions. All that an expert will do therefore is to enhance what you already know or have.

There is no substitute for hard work

It can be tempting sometimes to avoid hard work and put it aside for later. For a long time, you were used to the division of labor as an employee with others around ready to assist you with your chores. However, as an entrepreneur just getting started, you will have to work hard for a long time. This is crucial if you are to grow phenomenally, build your brand, and achieve your goals.

It is human nature to search for shortcuts to obtain quick results. While there are a couple of things that you can do in order to grow fast and obtain desired results, most things require that you put in the hard work and time. There is no substitute for the amount of hard work that it takes to grow and see long term success in business.

Regularly speak powerful words to yourself

Most things that we tell ourselves actually become a reality. As such, you need to speak positive words to yourself regularly. As human beings, when we convince ourselves using words that something is not possible, then it will most likely come to pass. Therefore, learn to tell yourself positive stories. Do this every day or as often as possible and ensure that you fill your mind and soul with positive words and thoughts.

You can say things such as how unstoppable you are and how you can accomplish anything that you set your mind to. Search and find web articles, blogs, videos, and podcasts that educate and motivate you. Also, make sure that you avoid negative individuals with low energy and people who drag you down. It's best to keep away from them because they can influence you negatively and slow you down. Try and obtain a vision of where you want to be and how you want your business to look like. Then keep working towards this vision and do not let anyone try to bring you down.

Avoid the shiny object syndrome

There is a phenomenon known as the Shiny Object Syndrome. This refers to the tendency of a person to abandon their current venture and pursue a new business goal or idea. This is a bad idea, and you should not pursue something new and relatively unknown instead of the business venture that you have planned and invested in for so long.

At its very core, the shiny object syndrome is known as the disease of distraction. This situation often affects entrepreneurs mostly due to their unique characteristics. You will find that entrepreneurs are mostly highly motivated individuals who desire new developments and have a passion for the latest technology. By nature, entrepreneurs do not have a fear of creating new things or starting new projects.

Generally, these characteristics of entrepreneurs are great. They are only troubling when the shiny object syndrome sets in. This situation is very similar to a small child chasing an object. Once they get the object and see what it is, they lose interest and immediately start pursuing something else. When it comes to entrepreneurs, they abandon their current venture and start pursuing new ventures. Avoid this syndrome and remain focused and dedicated to your dream and passion with your current venture.

Work, work, work and then work even harder

Remember that during the initial stages, you will need to put in a lot of hard work. This means working to develop your business. You will need to put in a lot of hard work. As such, you will need to be much disciplined. Do not accept to be waylaid and distracted from your business.

Building your business will be tough especially if you are ambitious and desire to reach the highest levels. You will put in money and lose, you will trust people and they will fail you, and you will generally suffer all manner of setbacks. Despite all these setbacks and challenges, you should persevere and keep on pushing.

A lot of successful entrepreneurs with million dollar empires today also went through similar challenges and suffered for lengthy periods of time. If you stay focused, keep your vision intact, and carry on working as hard as you can, victory will eventually come your way.

Hire a virtual assistant if necessary

Sometimes you may feel overwhelmed or have too much to do. In such cases, you may be unsure of what to do. You should never hesitate to seek help and ask for assistance. If you need help and decide to hire an assistant, then opt for a remote or virtual assistant. A virtual assistant is a much better option compared to a live, walk-in assistant.

A virtual assistant is able to accomplish a lot more because they operate remotely and do not need to spend any time commuting. A live assistant who works from your office is more expensive. Hiring one is also risky because personalities may clash.

Virtual assistants can help with much of your administrative tasks such as replying to emails, data entry, producing content for your social media pages, responding to social media posts and messages, and so much more. This will free you up to attend to more crucial matters such as processing sales and accounts.

There are plenty of places where you can find virtual assistants. These include platforms such as O-Desk, www.virtualassistants.com, Fivver.com, and many others. Once you find a suitable individual and agree on terms, you can proceed to assign them work and then do the rest of the work.

Chapter 2: Personal Branding and Branding for Business

Personal Branding

The term personal branding refers to the process of creating and developing an image or mark around your name and also your career. It also refers to promoting what you stand for and establishing what you believe in. A personal brand includes your unique experiences and skills that make you the unique individual that you are. When done professionally, personal branding will differentiate you from all other experts in your field. When you create a personal brand, you can use it to communicate and express your unique skills, values, and personality.

A brand can be anything

We are used to thinking that a brand can only be related to products or companies. For instance, major brands such as Apple, IBM, or Google are all associated with major companies. Things are a little different nowadays because just about anything can be branded. This includes individuals like you and me because as an individual, you can have a personal brand.

Basically, your personal brand includes what you are mostly known for. If you are a great photographer, an amazing actor, or funny comedian, then that will constitute part of your brand. This brand can exist both online and offline. There are plenty of tools available today that can help you to build and develop your brand. If you intend to create your own personal brand, then you should make use of these tools in order to create an outstanding impression on all those looking you up online.

It is possible for any person, any willing individual to create a brand and harness their power to be unique and stand out. This uniqueness can draw the public to your services and products or help you to get a message out. A personal brand is more about enabling you to present yourself so that the world can get to know who exactly you are and what it is that you have to offer.

Anyone can brand themselves

A personal brand is not something designated only for successful entrepreneurs or established individuals. It should be viewed as something that anyone can have. It will enable you to stand out from the rest. Developing a personal brand provides you with a proactive path of managing your career development and generally how others perceive you in the marketplace.

The very idea of developing a personal brand makes some people uncomfortable. However, you really should put your personal brand out there and take control of your image online. If you do not do this, then you are likely to lose out on numerous opportunities and getting others to control your image and narrative. Therefore, take the initiative and create your own brand and do not let others do it for you.

Personal branding matters

It is never too late to create your own personal brand. Some people might claim that the process is tedious and takes too much time. Others might think it is not worth your time. This is wrong because personal branding, as we have seen, is crucial for your success and presentation both online and offline. Yes, it will take up some time and effort but coming up with a personal brand is absolutely crucial.

People are searching for you over the internet

Regardless of your profession, career, age, it is advisable to create an online profile so people may actually know who you are. Even those seeking employment need a personal brand or an online presence. A prominent human resources organization claims that more than 50% of all employers will not employ anyone without an online presence.

As a fresh graduate or someone at the workplace seeking employment, you will be required to have an online presence or portfolio, and the best format is usually a personal brand. Therefore, take the time to organize and prepare a professional brand that will tell your story and let others know about your skills, talents, experiences, and achievements.

However, as a business person and entrepreneur, a personal brand is even more important. If you seek new opportunities or wish to engage with clients for business purposes, then you will need to have a personal brand. This way, your contacts will be able to see you and check you out if they ever need to just to know more about you.

Personal Branding and the Next Level

One of the most important reasons that should compel you to create a personal brand is to propel yourself forward. Your personal brand will help you take the next step and get ahead. You can consider your personal brand as an added channel for growing and promoting your success. It is an essential step when it comes to working towards achieving your goals.

Creating your brand may sometimes feel like a job

Creating your personal brand may sometimes feel like a daunting task. You may get the feeling that developing your profile is a lot of work. However, this work is essential if you are to have a brand and set it up both offline and online. The crucial part is developing the necessary content needed about your work, your life, and achievements. Once this is done, the rest will be easy and will flow smoothly. You will have established a firm foundation with a clear roadmap making the entire process a lot more manageable. A good personal brand will distinguish you from all the others. You can take control of the branding process by following these simple steps.

Effective Personal Branding Process

We have already established that a personal brand aims to present you as a very marketable, able, and capable brand. A lot of people do get overwhelmed when coming up with material for their brands. However, you should not panic if this happens. Simply take a deep breath and think about your achievements.

Brand building is an ongoing process and not a single event. You can break down the branding process into a number of phases. Even then, this is not a one-time incident and hence the reason why personal branding objectives and process look different for everyone. The process is broken down into three main segments. These pillars are:

- Designing a basic personal brand
- Getting an audience and building credibility
- Begin identifying opportunities

Building your personal brand

You need to first create a personal brand online that showcases your successes, qualifications, achievements, and so on. This way, should anyone search for you online, they will be able to come across a strong profile that showcases your strengths. To achieve this feat, you will need to first do the following:

- Audit your search engine results
- Any unsuitable content not fitting your image should be cleaned up
- Come up with a positive and suitable definition of yourself and brand
- Proceed to create an online presence that basically showcases your achievements, qualifications, and expertise

- Have a personal branding strategy to follow and observe the timelines

The first thing that you need to do before you begin building your brand is to search and find out what is out there. Use major search engines such as Google, Bing, and YouTube to learn what information is out there about you. There are tools that you can use to scan the internet search results for any potentially harmful information.

Should any risky information about you is out there, you should clean it up. You should take any necessary steps to get rid of the negative information. Any that you can delete, un-publish, and get rid of should be removed as soon as possible. You should also search across different websites and social media sites and find out what information is out there about you. Here is what you will need to get rid of:

- Drug use or beer drinking
- Unbecoming behavior
- Poor communication style
- Any polarizing views
- Criminal activity
- Sexual misconduct
- Bullying and violence

After cleaning up all the negative information out there, you will then begin the process of creating your own personal brand. Think about the kind of image that you want people to have of you. For instance, who are you as an individual and what qualities make you unique?

There are other factors that you need to consider. These include your personal branding goals, your professional achievements and ambitions, your audience and how you can build them, things that make you reliable and any evidence that is out there. If need be, you can search for individuals whose personal brands are out there and look similar to what you hope for.

1. Showcase your brand's strengths and achievements

There are ways of showcasing your skills and accomplishments. This is what should follow immediately after you have introduced yourself and presented your persona to the world. Showcase your strengths and achievements by:

- Listing moments when you were recognized your work and achievements
- Putting down the achievements and accomplishments you are proud of
- Think of other private achievements that were recognized

Spend some time and think about all these different situations and then come up with accurate and truthful answers for them all. List them down and make sure they are presentable. Think essentially about what impression you want to leave with anyone searching for you over the internet.

You will need to optimize your personal brand for search engines. If you do not know how to optimize for search engines, consider learning how to do it or hire someone else to do the optimization for you.

2. Build credibility

You will need to build some credibility into your personal brand in order to have placements in third-party websites and channels. After that, you can begin publishing content onto different sites, onto blogs, and all other places. To gain even further credibility, ensure that you post content on high-quality and respected sites.

Ensure that you write content and post it on different credible platforms. You can create different kind of content including blog articles, podcasts, audio clips, images, videos, infographics, and so much more. After posting your content, ensure that you keep track of your publications. Metrics are crucial if you are to keep track of your online performance. Therefore, keep track of all engagements that result from your content on various platforms.

Build an audience

You will need to have an online audience. The first step is to identify who and where your target is. What are the people interested in and what kind of content can I share with them? Once you identify your audience, you should find an influencer among them. This is an outstanding individual who can sway the opinion of your audience and has plenty of influence and say. The influence has the capacity of getting thousands of people to follow you and become the audience that you desire.

When it comes to an audience, you should start with those that you know. This means your friends and family as well as any other followers on your social media sites and email addresses list.

Finally, you will need to engage with your audience and nurture them so that you receive personal branding opportunities. Engage your audience with high quality, relevant, and useful content. Share this content with them and then engage all those who choose to comment, share, or otherwise engage your posts.

If you brand yourself properly, you could earn recognition as a thought leader in your industry. This will, in turn, provide you with numerous opportunities and open doors to possibilities that include interviews, speaking engagements, jobs, partnerships, membership, and a lot more.

Other Things to Enhance Your Personal Brand

Build a platform

Your online personal brand will need to be domiciled somewhere. As such, you are going to need a platform such as a website. Choose your names for your URL address. This will make it easier for others to find you should they search for you. Apart from a website, you will also require social media websites that represent your brand. Therefore, open up personal brand accounts on popular social media networks like Facebook, Twitter, Instagram, and others. Make use of these platforms to share your voice and put your brand out there.

Become a master in your chosen field

Your personal brand will generally paint you as an expert in one field or another. It will also prominently announce your unique strengths, qualifications, experiences, and talent. Learn how to own all these talents and become an expert in your field. Understand that you can never stop learning so keep listening, read a lot and learn as much as you can.

Share your knowledge

Becoming an expert and master in your chosen field is not enough. You need to share your knowledge with others. Therefore, ensure that you teach others, share ideas and showcase your immense wisdom. You can do this with your online audience and on your personal website using videos, podcasts, articles, and so on. Share your knowledge both online and offline.

Be yourself

Remember that you do not need to be anyone else but you. It is your unique personality and individual traits that will attract the kind of audience that you want. Basically, find your own unique style, stick with it, and set a path that others will surely follow.

Set your priorities and identify your values

You will need to then identify your priorities and values. An image of your professional and personal goals in the long and short terms should be clear by now. By doing this, you will be able to identify areas that you need to prioritize and spend more time on. Remember that you will use your priorities and values to guide you in your actions and in the decisions that you make.

Determine your brand persona

Now that you have a clearly defined brand, you will need to come up with a persona. There are a couple of things that you can use to create the persona. These include the following:

- Identify personality features and emotional appeal that you possess
- Describe yourself appropriately
- Clearly define your area of specialization

Make use of the above to come up with your unique persona. Remember that during the initial stages you will have to give and give then give some more before you can start taking. This means to give people ideas, share knowledge, provide useful and informative content and continue doing so until your community, followers, and customers trust you and consider you an expert in your chosen field.

More Things that Will Enhance Your Personal Brand

Even after putting up your personal brand both online and offline, you should take the time to learn a couple of new things. For instance, you should master money online skill. Such a skill will enhance your financial prowess and enable you to keep up with the business world.

Also, focus on building your social media presence. Social media has become a crucial platform for all business owners and renowned personalities. Building a social media following will take a while, but it is something that you can easily do at very little cost to yourself.

Ensure that you are in at least three or four of the major platforms. These include Instagram, YouTube, Facebook, Pinterest, Twitter, and LinkedIn. Doing so will get your personal brand out there with the opportunity to come across billions of social media users. Start a podcast or a YouTube channel and keep it active. Add fresh content regularly. Ensure that you teach those around you. Coach them regularly and help to enhance their success.

You will have to remain alert and watch the performance of your business. Provide free information, tips, advice, and guidance to others, including your followers and general audience. Let them learn to count on you as leader and guru in your chosen field. This way, they will eventually get to trust you and listen to your every word.

At this stage, you will still need to give, give, and then give some more. Keep providing informative blogs and articles, share informative and relevant videos and all other content. It is only after giving so much of yourself and gaining the trust of thousands of followers will you be successful at converting them into paying customers.

Chapter 3: Important Networking Strategies

As you work hard to grow and market your business, you will need to invest in networking. If you are well connected, you will be able to find exactly what you need with just a couple of phone calls. Networking will help to save you time because the right people and resources will always be within easy reach whenever you need them.

Good networking will also bring in clients effortlessly as you will not need to work as hard as others if you apply the best networking strategies. Even then, you can waste a lot of time if you do not network the right way. Business networking is all about being strategic and focusing on your goals.

While most people focus on online networking, you will achieve much better success by meeting people face-to-face. This is because online networking is nowhere near as effective as in-person networking. Here are some effective networking strategies that you can adapt to enhance your business and personal brand

Change your networking strategy

There are plenty of business owners who make plenty of mistakes trying to network as they are often desperately trying to earn an income. Do not focus on how to push your agenda, get all the attention to yourself and possibly manipulate and impress others. Instead think what you can offer others, be helpful and see to their success. Focus on starting and holding friendly conversations and putting others at ease. Basically just think about being sincere, helping others and being generous.

Clearly define your goals

You need to clearly know and understand the reasons why you are networking. People network for numerous reasons. Are you searching for new business connections, new clients, or friends and mentors? Make sure that you closely interact with positive influencers. Also, try and surround yourself with successful individuals who are where you want to be. Ask them lots of questions and learn as much as you can from them.

Previously, business owners and managers focused on networking in order to acquire new clients. This approach never worked out well. However, when the focus changed on finding suitable partners and mentors, then clients came their way. Therefore, focus on finding motivational and inspirational business leaders, influencers, and mentors and the rest will follow.

Get out there and make a great expression

You do not need to waste time. When it comes to networking, you need to get out there and start meeting exciting and amazing individuals. There are always events happening in your town or nearby towns. Find trade shows and networking events that will assist you in achieving your networking goals.

Book events in advance and pay if they charge a fee. Once at the event, have your business cards ready. This is important because you will be able to reach out to others and create a great impression. Make sure that you look your best at these events so that you create a lasting impression. For instance, you can choose your clothes the night before, so they are ready in the morning.

Have your follow up questions ready as well as your elevator pitch. Remember that networking is all about follow-up. Therefore, keep in touch with all the useful contacts that you made. Keep track of all the people in your network and the kind of things you discussed. The difference between meeting your networking goals and missing them depends on follow up.

Essential Networking Strategies

Whether you are an entrepreneur or corporate executive, you will need to develop your networking skills. Networking is crucial because as a small business owner, your clients will consist mostly of referrals from within your network. In fact, referrals often constitute 80% – 90% of all business revenues for small businesses. Here are some skills and strategies you will need to develop if you are to be successful.

Learn to develop a thick skin

You will need to learn how to take "no" for an answer. This will require plenty of patience on your part. If you can be polite and develop a thick skin, then you will fare much better.

Be nice to those you meet

It is important that you learn to be nice to everyone you encounter. This is because you never know when you will need. Sometimes the people you encounter as you build your network or go about your business might come in handy should things get difficult.

Become a great communicator

You should maintain regular interactions with the people in your network or database. You should also work to grow your relationships because most of the time you will be 4 to 5 relationships away from what you want.

One of the best ways of maintaining communication is to meet face-to-face with the people in your database or network. Maintaining consistent and regular contact with individuals within your network is a successful way of communicating. When you are unable to meet in person, then make phone calls or leave personal notes.

Keep it simple

Focus on where most of your resources are being spent especially your energy and time. Think about the kind of results that you want to have. Are you getting these results? Where you see results is where you need to spend your resources. You should not spend your precious time or energy on things that bring no returns.

Gain access to the available resources

Today you can access plenty of resources that can help you with your networking strategies. There are lots of books that you can read. Also build strong relationships with friends, family, and colleagues. Also, join networking groups both online and in person. Make sure that you get connected and stay connected.

Always remember that networking is all about interacting with people, sharing information, nurturing relationships, and expanding your contacts. It helps you build relationships, learning about career opportunities, and so much more. Networking is really a life skill that every entrepreneur should have. It helps to build, maintain, and nurture mutually-beneficial relationships that will last for years to come.

When it comes to networking those who are good at storytelling will emerge winners. Learn how to tell your story and when to tell it. Think about what you want to share and who you want to share it with. People want to hear about your business, about your dream, and about your possible humble beginnings. However, learn how to tell your story, so it is interesting, inspirational, memorable, and entertaining. However, narrate your story in as few words as possible. People may not have all the time to listen to long, unending stories.

Chapter 4: Online Networking Strategies

One of the best ways of presenting your brand to the public and anyone who searches for you to know you better is through a personal blog. If you optimize your blog appropriately using the right keywords and other SEO techniques, then your blog will be really easy to find. Anyone searching for you on the internet using search engines will easily find you.

What is a Blog?

A blog can be defined as a website whose content is produced by an individual. A blog focuses mostly on written content, and the author is often the owner of the blog. Blogs are actually, and the content is known as blog posts. Most of us have probably heard about celebrity blogs and news blogs. However, blogs are not exclusive only to the rich and powerful in society. Anyone can have their own blog.

You can successfully start your own blog and write just about anything that you like. People who write blogs are popularly referred to as bloggers, usually write from a personal perspective. This way, they are able to connect with their readers quite easily. Most blogs also allow readers to leave comments in a comments section. This section appears right after the main blog content. It is advisable to enable your readers to interact with you.

Letting your audience share their opinions and responding to their comments is crucial as it helps to build the connection between the blogger and his or her readers.

In fact, one of the most important aspects of starting a blog is the interaction between the blog owner and his or her readers. This interaction and connection enable you to share information, knowledge, ideas, and matters of general interest with your audience.

Why You Need to Start Your Own Blog

Blogging has very quickly turned out to be among the best ways of spreading news and information as well as communicating. There are essentially millions of blogs across the internet on different subjects, topics, and personalities. Different people from across different nations log onto the internet to find content to read and use. Therefore starting your own blog will open doors for you and enable you to share your profile and any other information that you want.

You should also start a blog because blogging affords you an opportunity to share information with others and to freely express your thoughts and feelings about different issues that are crucial to your or your community. And when you begin writing your blog, you generally become a much better person as well as a better and more improved writer. And the best part about blogging is that you can promote your personal brand, your business, and even make money in the process. Numerous bloggers across America and around the world are earning money from their blogs.

Other Things You Can Do with Your Blog

Earn a passive income: There are other things that you can do with your blog. You can, for instance, make money using your blog. While your income may not compare to some of the top bloggers in the world, you can earn a decent income each week or month. If you learn how to blog and do it the right way, then you will be able to establish a rewarding side gig. A passive income is the desire of numerous people across the globe. Earning an income while doing something else is like a dream come true. For instance, you can spend just a couple of hours per week writing your blog but earn hundreds of dollars within that same week.

Share your story: One of the best ways of presenting yourself to the world and sharing your story is via a blog. It gives you a voice with which to express yourself and your thoughts so that others may get to know more about you. Many writers use blogs to talk about their daily experiences and so much more. This way, they let in others into their lives and also share with others close to them and allowing them to be part of their lives.

Express your personal and business brands: You can use your blog to express your personal brand and your business brands as well. Blogs are extremely effective at this. Apart from your website, a blog is one of the best places online to express your personal brand and put it out there for others to view. If you are seeking recognition among your peers and other professionals in your chosen industry, then a blog is the platform to use.

Identify a suitable community to relate with: We have noted that blogs are inherently interactive platforms. Whenever you post a blog, your followers and viewers will read it and then leave comments at the very end. This provides an excellent platform to interact with others and generally build a community of like-minded individuals with shared interests. You get to teach your followers and share useful information with them. In the end, they will respect you and your opinions and consider you a guru and expert in your field.

Creating Your Own Blog

There are plenty of misconceptions about blogs. For instance, there is a presumption that you have to be a really great writer or trained journalist in order to become a successful blogger. This is not necessarily true because people from walks of life read blogs every day. They do so in search of content that they find suitable and that is of interest to them.

Another thing is that you do not have to write formally at all. In fact, most bloggers are successful because of their casual and informal style of blogging. As an example, people who read blogs about cars do not want to read from an engineer or technician. They would rather read from a fellow motorist with real-life experience.

Have a passion for your topic

To be a successful blogger, there is only one requirement, and that is to have a lot of passion for your chosen niche. Blogging is really all about sharing your thoughts, experiences, ideas, dreams, and hopes. The platform gives you a chance to express yourself and have your content read by thousands and maybe millions of internet users.

You get to choose the topic that you want to write about and then talk about it as passionately as possible. When you do this, you will stand a high chance of success. Essentially, when you choose the kinds of topics that you want to write about, you will succeed because of the passion you have on the topics.

Getting started with your blog

By this point, you are ready to start your own blog. However, where exactly do you begin and what tools or equipment do you require? Here are some basic and easy steps that you can follow.

Questions you need to ask before getting started:

What are you passionate about? This is the most important question to ask yourself. If you have no passion for a topic, then simply do not write, or blog, about it. Passion is an essential ingredient for successful blogging. It will keep you motivated and will prevent you from giving up.

You will be able to develop your skill sets in a particular niche if you are passionate about it. Another reason why passion is important is that if it is lacking, then your readers will pick up on it. And if you do not care, your readers will take off.

Is your preferred niche profitable? It is important to consider the financial benefit your blog could bring. While a lot of people blog because it is something they enjoy doing, it should be profitable as well, for long term sustainability.

Also, consider the fact that it takes quite a while before your blog starts earning you an income. Some of the things you need to keep in mind when you ask this question include your resources, ease of attracting advertisers, whether others are making money in this niche, and what the competition is like. You can use search engines such as Google to find competitors in your niche.

If you want to earn a decent income regularly through your blog, then you need to truly understand whether you can make lots of money in your preferred niche. It is just not worth it spending the next 12 months trying to make money and failing eventually.

Is your niche viable? The truth is that some niches are too small to be viable and growth will eventually climax at a point. From thereon it will be a struggle to increase your traffic, and you will probably run out of content ideas. When considering a niche, you may want to use some keyword tools to get an idea of how many people are searching for a particular keyword.

Some of the keyword research tools that you can use include Google Keyword Planner, Long Tail Pro, and SEM Rush. Even then, the figures you obtain are merely estimates that will guide you in arriving at a decision. Also, look at the competition. If your niche has competition, then it probably is a worthwhile niche. However, if the competition is quite strong and able, then you could run into difficulty because competition may just be too strong.

What does the public really need? It is important that you consider factors such as the importance of your niche to the general public, or specifically, your readers. People have different needs, and according to Maslow's Hierarchy of Needs, there are some needs that are definitely more important than others. For instance, food and water are basic needs which are essential. Video games, on the other hand, are only optional.

Do you need some niche ideas? If you need to get ideas about your blog, then you can find plenty of blogs with ideas. Consider checking out Amazon Best Seller list.
Amazon is one of the most trusted retailers in the world, and this is why simply recommending a product on Amazon can lead to more people purchasing it. The Amazon bestseller list covers all categories that there are. Categories include hot new releases, top rated, and many others.

Choose a name for your blog

Your blog has to have a name. This will be your first task. Therefore, take some time and think about the kind of name that you want for your blog. If you have an idea about what name you'd like for your blog then go ahead and use that name. However, if you really got no idea, then use some resources from the internet to help you come up with a suitable one.

Passion and hobbies: One of the best ways of coming up with a blog name is to work within your hobby or passion. Common passions and hobbies that people have include fashion, cars, sports, travel, and cooking. However, your blog could also be about other less common things such as seafood or Persian culture. There is always an audience for any niche that you choose so follow your passion and you will eventually be successful.

Life experiences: Some people want to write blogs about their own personal experiences. They probably have learned useful lessons which they wish to share with their readers. If you have gone through certain experiences, then sharing this information on your blog will definitely help some of your readers.

Think about some of the extraordinary experiences that you have had. You can write about these and help others with advice.

A personal blog: As a business leader and entrepreneur, you need to have your own personal blog. This is a blog that will showcase your personality, your strengths, achievements, hopes, and future outlook. You can also write about other different topics on your personal blog including a variety of things that you regularly do. Such a platform provides an excellent way of sharing your thoughts with the rest of the world.

Name your blog

It is advisable to choose a descriptive name for your blog. This way, potential readers and visitors from across the web can instantly find out what your blog is all about from its name.

If you intend to write a blog about a particular subject or topic, then ensure that you include this subject within your blog name in some way. Let us assume you want to write about food. You do not necessarily have to include food in the name, but related terms such as recipe, cooking, or meals will do just fine.

For personal blogs, it is best to use your own name because you will probably be writing about lots of different topics. You could also use a variation of your names in a way that will identify the blog as a personal one. There are plenty of different name variations that you could use. Think about all these variations then come up with one that you believe is the most suitable for your blog.

Choose a domain extension

As soon as you decide on your preferred blog name, you will need to choose a domain name. The most preferred in this case is a .com. However, others such as .org and .net are also acceptable. Once you have the complete blog name including extension, you should check and confirm that it is indeed available. If you are fortunate enough and the name is available, then you can go ahead and use it. However, if it is not, then you can try different variations until you find one that is available.

Get your blog online

Now that your blog has both a name and an extension, you need to get it online. This process is not as technical as you may think and can be achieved if you understand what needs to be done. Here is how to go about it.

The first step to getting your blog online requires two things. These are blogging software and a host. The best part is that these often come packaged together. Therefore, identify a good host that is providing suitable and affordable services and have them host your blog. Remember that you must have a blog host if you are to have a blog and get it online. The host will not just provide hosting services but will also provide you with the software that you need to actualize your blog.

There are plenty of web hosts that you can use. A good one will provide you with a number of services including registering your blog name so that no one else uses it. Your host should provide you with free and very simple-to-use software. The most common software is WordPress. This software currently hosts more than 2 million websites and blogs. Once you sign up with one of these hosting sites, the software will be installed and you can then begin working on your blog.

Customize your blog

To get you started, you will need to first log into your account. Use the host's software such as WordPress and log in there. From here you can begin customizing your website, so it looks as neat and beautiful or presentable as you like. There are plenty of options available for you. They range from free to paid profiles to add-ons, images that you can use for your blog, formats, and layouts.

Most blogging software is designed with users in mind. This means that the software is generally easy to use and requires little or no training. You may require a couple of lessons to learn the basics through tutorials. Once you learn these, then you should be able to comfortably use the software and customize your blog as you want. You can find tutorials on YouTube and on the internet should you wish to get further information about how to use the software.

All these changes and options are available to you from the administration page. This page allows you to manage and oversee your blog website the way you want it. Most people have different ideas about how they want their blogs to look. Appearance is apparently very important. This is why the software provided has so many options when it comes to themes, layouts, and so on.

As soon as the theme is installed, you can activate your blog by clicking on the "Activate" blog. It's easy at this stage to view your blog's theme and appearance. Simply enter the URL address into your browser and then take a look. If you want to make a difference, then you can do so through the administration page of your software. Now that your blog is ready, it is time to start writing and publishing content.

Writing and Publishing Blog Posts

Now that your blog is up and running, you need to start writing content and publishing it. This is easy to do. When you log onto your blog, you will find a default blog there. This is okay, and you can always delete it. You can now proceed to write your very first blog. You can do so directly on the site or offsite on a word processor such as MS Word then transfer and publish it on your blog.

Remember that you are free to write just about anything that you like, especially if yours is a personal blog. However, if it is a topical blog where you write content within a specific niche, then focus on matters within that industry. If you are happy with your post, then feel free to publish it as soon as you are ready. If there are any changes that need to be made, then make those changes before publishing the post.

You may realize after publishing your post that it does not look appealing on its own and would look much better with a photo or image. If you want to add an image, you will first need to ensure that you find a suitable one which does not violate any copyright laws. Once your image is ready, you simply need to publish it using the button provided. Now that you have your content ready, take a look at it and rectify any errors or mistakes. If it is perfect according to you, then it is ready for publishing.

Choosing blogging topics

As a blogger, you will often be advised to blog about a topic or niche you are passionate about. While there is some truth to this statement, the best advice would be to tell you about the best niches you should consider. This is if you really want a large audience, be influential, and earn a lot of money.

If you are to be a successful blogger, then you should think about blogging with a purpose. This increases your market share, revenue growth, consumer engagement, and of course, a return on your investment. Blogging with a purpose applies whether you operate a business or not. The aim here is to be a successful blogger.

Problem choosing niches

There is a problem that many bloggers face and this is choosing the wrong niche for your blog. There are a number of reasons why a particular niche could be wrong for you.

Passion: It could be that you are not passionate enough about a particular niche or topic. Perhaps you do not understand it well enough, or it could be a difficult one. Plenty of people have spent a lot of money and time blogging the wrong niche only to realize this about a year or so later.

Money: Some bloggers set out to simply make money. Such a blogger picks on a niche they believe will make them a lot of money. A couple of months or years later, they realize they have no zeal or passion for the niche, and so they begin losing followers. Basically, when your heart is not into something, your audience will realize, and they will start leaving in droves.

You also could be passionate about a niche, but then blogging does not make you any money. While having passion is great, making money is equally important. The financial strain that may result when you don't make any money could lead to serious challenges, and you may eventually be forced to quit blogging.

As a blogger, you need sufficient passion and drive to keep going. You also need to be able to earn plenty of money from your blog to provide you with the financial freedom that you always wanted. There are a good number of people who are earning six-figure incomes annually merely from blogging. There is no reason why this should not be you.

Chances are that the decision of which niche to blog about could affect the next five to ten years of your life especially if you are in it for the long haul. To be successful, you have to take every little factor into account.

Publishing the Blog

Now that you are ready to showcase your blog and share your post with the world, all you need to do is to publish the blog. First, click the "publish" button then go to your software page and take a look. Find the "Launch" button so that your blog is launched officially on the web. When this happens, then your blog will be published on the internet and will be available to anyone who wants to read your posts. Congratulations! Your blog is now live!

Promote the Blog

Now that your beautifully designed website with excellent content has been published you need to promote it so that people get to know about it. You should keep in mind that writing and publishing a website as well as creating and designing a blog are just the initial steps. Without promoting the blog and letting others know about will mean that all your work was in vain.

There are millions of published websites that are published but are never viewed or read by anyone. This is because people are unaware about the existence of the blog. You will have to promote your blog and let everyone get to find out about its existence. This means taking proactive steps to advertise the blog and letting as many people as possible know about your website and what they can expect to find.

Promote your blog on social media

One of the best ways of promoting your website is to use your social media accounts. If you have an account or presence on the popular social media websites such as Facebook, Twitter, Instagram, and so on, then you can use these to promote the blog. First, you should post your blog's link onto your social media pages, so interested followers and friends can follow the link and read your blog.

One of the benefits of using your social media accounts is that there are plenty of people you know on these sites. Most of these people are probably your friends or following you. Share the link with them and let them learn about your blog's existence. These friends and followers are likely to share your link with others so that there is a multiplier effect. This means that more and more people will view your blog and read your posts. If you do create high-quality blogs, then you have a high chance of attracting a huge audience within a short period of time.

Another form of promotion that you will need to work on is to retain your readers. Basically, you will want all your readers to come back after reading your initial post. As such, you will need to maintain contact with these visitors. The best way to do this is to collect email addresses. This is easy to do because you can collect email addresses of your readers.

Email marketing

There is a tool that you can install on your blog to politely request email addresses of your visitors. Use this email tool to collect and create a list of interested followers and readers. Once you have a list of emails, then you can use them for email marketing. This means sending regular email messages to your followers whenever you publish a blog. Your followers will be happy to receive updates and notices whenever something new is published. This is way more important than you might think, so make sure you build your email list. Realize that no one can take this from you and it's another way to market to your customers.

Since you will keep in contact with your followers via email and blog, you will be able to develop a closer relationship with them. When you develop a closer relationship with your followers, they will trust in you, and they can easily become your customers should you create a business.

Comment on other blogs

Another way of advertising and promoting your blog is to read other blogs and leave comments on the posts. When you comment on these posts, leave behind comments and provide useful information and feedback. Try and paint yourself as an expert on the subject matter then guide other readers to your blog by including a link back to your blog or to a specific post.

Other readers on these other blogs will see your comments and will likely follow the link back to your website. Please keep in mind that this is a great opportunity for you to put your blog right in the face of numerous other readers. Make sure that you are polite and very professional and you will attract a lot of additional viewers.

It is advisable to focus on popular blogs with hundreds of thousands of readers and followers. These include platforms such as Quora and others. These sites receive millions of visitors each day. You can tap into this viewership and attract as many of these viewers as possible. This way, you will enjoy additional visitors to your blog.

Guest posting

Yet another way of popularizing your blog is through posting content on other blogs and websites as a guest. There are numerous places all over the internet where you can post your content and share it there. Many websites invite guests to post on their blogs so take the time to contact the owners of these blogs and ask to post. This happens all the time so you will have numerous opportunities. However, not all bloggers welcome guests to post on their blogs. Therefore, make sure that you contact willing blog owners and then proceed to create high-quality content on their blogs. Make sure that you also include links that lead back to your website. If people love your writing and enjoy your content, then they will definitely visit your website and will become avid followers. This is yet another way of providing you with new followers and readers. You can then collect their contacts and email address for your mailing list.

Monetize your Blog

Did you know that you can make money through your blog? Apparently, a blog provides you with an excellent opportunity to make money on a regular basis. This kind of income is known as passive income because you only work a few hours each week while earning money regular from your venture. It is important to understand that there are various ways of making money and earn a profit through activities on your blog.

There are things that can earn you a profit. These include providing services and selling products to your clients and generally selling to the general public. If you have a good product or a quality service, then you can sell it and make a profit. However, there is an even easier way of making money from your blog, and this is through the sale of advertising space. By selling advertising space, you will make money on a regular basis this way.

If your readership increases with more people reading your posts, then numerous advertisers will seek you out and offer you money for advertising space. One of the best providers of advertising opportunities is Google AdSense. Google will find advertisers for you and sell space on your behalf. Therefore, seek out Google AdSense and place the code on your blog. Once you do this, you will not need to struggle with finding advertisers because Google will do all the hard work on your behalf.

Monetize your blog through affiliate programs

If you want to make money through blogging, then one of the best ways to do this is through affiliate marketing. There are plenty of affiliate marketing programs available. As an affiliate marketer, your job will be to first attract interested persons to your website through the content that you produce and then redirect these visitors onto a third party website to a particular product and service. If they purchase the product or pay for a service, then you will receive a commission.

The process is really simple. First, you need to find a suitable affiliate program. Not all programs out there are suitable for find one that is. One of the best affiliate programs is offered by Amazon and is known as Amazon Affiliates.

You can also consider affiliate aggregator services. There are firms out there that actually provide aggregation services to blogs like yours if you write on a diverse range of topics. In general, you will need to come up with high-quality content that actually sells. This is not hard to do if you are passionate about your niche. Take your time to research information and then present in a manner that everyone can read and understand. Use affiliate advertising only as an additional resource.

Remember to maintain a reader-friendly environment within your blog. Your readers come to your blog primarily to read your blogs and possibly leave comments. Keep it that way for the most part. It is important that you maintain a balance between actual blogging and monetization. User experience must be kept high otherwise your readers may be bombarded with marketing messages and disappear.

SEO: Search Engine Optimization for your Blog and Website

The term SEO stands for search engine optimization, and it refers to all the activities necessary to optimize your website or blog for search engines. When you have a blog or website, you want anybody searching for you using search engines to be able to find you. If you do not optimize your blog, then no one will probably ever come across it, and it may as well not exist.

In fact, any person with a blog or website should optimize it, or it does not exist. Apparently, over 80% of web users start their internet browsing on search engines. You want them to find your blog if they are searching for content or information relevant to your industry. Basically, SEO will help you get the reach that you want. If you wish to reach out to a large following, then focus on the keywords that will enable you to do that.

Since you have a blog, you need to know that content writing is crucial for every SEO strategy. You need to develop high-quality content for your readers on a regular topic. If you do this, then you will be enhancing your chances of getting found by internet users searching within your industry.

Keywords

Your content should also contain the necessary keywords. According to experts, your optimization process should begin with keyword research. It is crucial that you figure out the most important keywords that you should use with each post. Learning how to do keyword research is essential because you need to identify the correct keywords for your post. Use the keywords that you want to rank for. For instance, if you are writing about exotic birds, then use keywords affiliated with exotic birds. These could include tropical parrots, African owls, and so on.

On-page SEO

There are a couple of techniques that you can apply to your blog page. These are the on-page techniques that you need to focus on. The first is the URL link. You need to optimize this link appropriately. Use the topic of your post as part of the URL. This way, you will not only optimize the page but will make it easier for anyone to know what your page is all about. For instance, if your blog is about exotic birds and you are writing a post about "Tropical birds in Mauritius," then your URL would look something like www.exoticbirds.com/tropical-birds-in-Mauritius.

You should also maintain the correct keyword density. The best ratio for optimum keyword density is 2%. If you use fewer keywords, your search engine ranking will be lower, but if you use too many, then you will be penalized by the search engines for keyword stuffing. Therefore, be careful with your keywords. If you get it right then, your blog will rank highly, but if not, your rankings will be affected.

You need to learn where to place keywords. As an SEO expert, you should use your keywords on the heading, the title, the first line of your post and the last line. Sometimes it is advisable to use the keyword somewhere in the body of your post. In many cases, bloggers use more than one keyword. In such cases, then you should designate one of them as the main keyword. The rest will be additional or other keywords. Remember to observe the 2% keyword density rule for posts, not more than 500 words.

Other SEO formatting requirements

To improve your SEO, you will need to do additional optimization. These include formatting your images for SEO. Images have titles so optimize these titles. If there are any related links, then optimize these as well.

You need to make use of Meta tags. A Meta tag is a generated HTML tag that enables search engines to recognize the description, title, and additional information about a URL. These do have a slight impact on keywords, therefore, make use of them.

Also crucial to have are Meta descriptions. This is a brief description of a blog or website that described briefly what the blog is all about. It is often not more than three lines long and appears after a search is conducted.

Comment section

Your blog will most likely have a comment section where readers are free to leave comments based on the post they just read. There are readers who like to leave comments together with an external link. This is ok as it is allowed. However, you need to block search engines from crawling through that particular link.

You should also format the comments section. You need to moderate this section to prevent spam comments and things like that. When replying to comments from your readers try and make use of your keywords as well. This will help boost your ranking as well.

Finally, remember that the bottom line and the most important part of your blog is the post. This means that the content needs to be top quality without any compromise. Your readers and all other visitors to your blog will appreciate quality content that is beautifully written, interesting to read, and informative. SEO should not distract you from the readability of your post. If you follow these basic tips, you will end up with a high-quality blog post that is aptly optimized for search engines, making it easy for web users to find and read.

Chapter 5: Social Media Marketing and Advertising

Introduction to Social Media Marketing

The term social media is a general term that refers to totally different websites that provide platforms for social actions. For instance, Facebook is a website and social network that enables users to share photos, updates, videos, stories, links and so much more. On the other hand, Twitter is yet another social network even though it is drastically different from Facebook. It essentially allows users to share short snippets, links, and updates.

Social media marketing provides a powerful avenue for businesses of all sizes to access and address customers and prospects. Most customers are on social media already and are interacting with lots of other brands. Therefore, if you are not reaching out to them via social media, then you are losing out big time. Using social media for marketing purposes is bound to bring you remarkable success. You will be able to create an amazing and respected brand and even drive sales and leads.

Getting Started with Marketing

You do not need to be a rocket scientist to be a successful marketer. However, you do need a sound strategy if you are to be successful in your campaigns. There is no single marketing solution for all businesses. Each small business is different from all others. Therefore, you need to come up with a marketing strategy that is best suited for your business.

The nature of your business really does not matter. This is because all businesses need to have a marketing strategy. Therefore, whether you have a consulting business, a café, an auto garage, a grocery store, or a consignment shop, you will need to find ways to bring in customers to your business. If you are to be successful in your endeavors, then you need to understand the process of deciding on a plan, sticking with the plan, and applying the same resources and time needed.

The marketing process

1. Get the know-how: The very first thing that you need to do is acquire the know-how regarding marketing. As a business owner, you really need to know exactly what to do because marketing can be a tricky path to navigate. Having the skills and knowledge on how to conduct a successful marketing campaign is crucial. Therefore, take the time to acquire marketing skills that will enable you to market your business and products effectively.

2. Set goals and plan a budget: Now that you have the necessary knowledge that you need to define your end goal then come up with a suitable budget. You really need to know exactly what you want. For instance, if you sell products, you will want these products to get to a certain niche in the market. When customers buy your products, you will make a profit. Therefore, think about what is important to your business and how far you want to extend your reach. Remember to prioritize your goals by defining your most crucial needs and your long-term endeavors.

Marketing is also a numbers game. You need to set attainable goals and have ways of measuring your success. You also need to ensure that you only engage in efforts that will directly or indirectly bring results. Efforts that do not bring in new business are of no use to you. Therefore, have well-defined goals in terms of profit, revenue, costs, new sales and number of inquiries. These will help you to keep a tab on your marketing efforts.

3. Identify your target market: One of the most important steps you will need to make is to identify who your target market is. Apparently, not anyone who is walking and talking is your target market. To determine the demographic that constitutes your market, you need to do a few things including market research and conducting surveys. The data you receive from these processes will then be analyzed, and the information will point you in the right direction. You will be able to determine who your target market is and in what niche they are in. It will then be possible to craft or design a marketing campaign around your market niche and target audience.

4. Marketing is more than just advertising: There are numerous aspects to marketing and not just posting adverts or creating websites. If you own a small business, you will have numerous ways of marketing your business beyond advertising. It will benefit you greatly if you find out which marketing tactics work and which ones are not suitable for your niche. Eliminate the ones that do not work so you do not waste any unnecessary funds, time, and effort on them.

5. Put your customers first: You need to take time and really get to know who your customers are. When you get to understand them and know what it is that they really value and want, then you will be well on your way towards a successful marketing campaign. Even after you get new customers, you need to keep in touch with them after the sales and let them understand that you are concerned about their welfare. Try and ensure that you stay ahead of the competition by putting your customers' needs first.

6. You have to spend in order to earn: As a marketer and entrepreneur, you need to understand the principle that you have to spend in order to earn. Basically, nothing comes out of nothing. In order to gain customers and make sales, you will need to spend some money. Marketing is a huge task, and you will need sufficient funds in order to finance these tasks. However, you will reap profits out of your efforts if you spend money where necessary.

7. Make use of social media: A lot of consumers today are on one social media or another. Social media has become so popular that people use it almost on a daily basis for different purposes. Some seek information while others look to share information and news items. Many others wish to find entertainment and anything of interest. Learn how to make use of social media and make sure that it becomes a major aspect of your marketing campaigns.

How Social Media Marketing Helps with Marketing Goals

The best part about social media is that it can be your business' best friend. You can use it adequately to achieve a couple of goals. These goals include some of the following:

- Increasing brand awareness
- Building and enhancing conversions
- Increasing web traffic
- Creating a positive brand association and identity
- Enhancing interaction and communication with an audience

Basically, the larger and more engaged your social media audience is, the easier things will be for you. This will ensure that you achieve most of all your marketing goals. There are numerous social media websites out there. You can use one or more of these websites for effective marketing campaigns. We will now examine some of the more popular social media sites one at a time.

Facebook Advertising

Facebook is the world's largest and most widely used social networking websites. Statistics show that there are more than 2.2 billion users around the world using this popular social site. This massive global audience means that Facebook is a powerful marketing platform for just about all businesses.

If you are a small business owner, an aspiring entrepreneur, or any other enterprise, then you should take advantage of the massive opportunities provided on this social media platform to market their services or brands and leverage this powerful resource for massive profitability.

Paid advertising on Facebook

There are many different ways of reaching out to consumers on Facebook. One of these is by simply opening a page or creating a profile. You can then invite friends and others that you know, so they join you and follow you. After that, you can share content and leverage or harness the power of Facebook to invite more followers.

Posts and powerful content are other examples of Facebook marketing techniques. You can share content of all kind with your followers and then ask your social media followers and friends to share your content. If you have a brand and products or a service to offer, you can post images and share content and links about this service and let others know.

All these are effective solutions for Facebook. However, they will not get you very far because your reach is limited. Fortunately, we have Facebook ads. Paid advertising on this platform provides one of the most trusted ways of reaching out to followers and interested persons within a niche or industry. You can pay for Facebook ads and use them to achieve certain aims. These could be increasing your reach, advertising your brand, or even searching for customers.

Targeted Facebook ads

Facebook has certain powerful features that make ads very effective. Micro-targeting is one such feature. Using micro-targeting, you can reach out to numerous users all at the same time. If you wish to reach, for instance, American males between ages 25 – 45 living in Madison, Wisconsin, then Facebook can help you attain this kind of reach.

Facebook ads enable you to reach your desired target audience according to interests, location, demographics, and sometimes even behavior. Basically, you are able to reach out to the exact kind of people you think are most receptive to your business, message, brand, and products. A lot of people are making money out of Facebook ads.

Targeted ads are beneficial because they enable you to reach out your preferred audience at very low prices. Traditional ads are very expensive and are never targeted at a specific or desirable group. As such, these ads are great for conversion rates, excellent for your budget, and you get a good return of investment.

Facebook ads actually charge you to reach out only to your most valuable followers and most potential customers. However, there is not one type of advertisement only but several. It is crucial to understand all about Facebook ads and exactly how they work. There is an entire process involved ranging from planning your very fast ad to more advanced techniques and advertising strategies.

Facebook is definitely the platform where your business should be. This is because of the numerous users as well as the great business opportunities the platform affords you. However, many other businesses are also on Facebook battling for the same opportunities. Facebook organic reach has been declining in the past couple of years, so a proper strategy, in this case, is necessary. Here are some tips on how to skyrocket your traffic reach.

Use content that is optimized to generate shares and attract attention

For successful social media experience and increased reach, you should consider using highly sharable content. Such content is the kind that causes users scrolling down the timeline to pause and read your post. Such posts should be so inspiring that readers feel a strong need to share with their followers. You will be rewarded handsomely for your engaging content by Facebook.

Try and post less content

A lot of time, Facebook users believe that more is better. However, people do not like being overwhelmed with content and posts on the timeline. It is crucial to understand the importance of tidbit information. There are those who believe you must post over 30 times each month and share over 5000 links in order to get ahead. In reality, less is more, and it is better. Post fewer items but ensure the ones that you do post are of excellent quality.

Increase engagement by boosting your best posts

If you wish to get more traffic from Facebook, then you really need to reach more of your followers. One of the ways of doing this is by boosting your best posts. For starters, you have to produce top-notch content. This is necessary if you are to see any major results. You should expect your traffic to skyrocket if you can create engaging content that is of high quality.

Combine Facebook ads with email and target repeat visitors

If you wish to drive Facebook traffic to your website, then you can use this indirect method for success. You will need to have the right audience for this. Basically, you will first provide a simple way for Facebook users to join your email list. The button to join the mailing list is very visible, and the process takes only a few seconds.

Give audience engagement priority

As a business owner, you should seize every opportunity that you get to engage your audience. The reason is that personal engagement is what keeps them coming back. You need to maintain polite, casual engagement and then share or like their posts. When your followers or other Facebook users leave a comment, this is a way of engaging you in conversation. Make sure to respond to their comment and keep the engagement going. When your audience feels that they are being heard and their opinions matter, they will engage you even further and will become loyal followers and possibly customers.

Different types of Facebook ads

1. Photo ads

One of the best ways of getting started is through photo advertisements. They are easy to design and post and take a very short while to prepare. You are able to come up with a photo ad and use it for various purposes such as to boost an existing post on your page. Photo ads are fairly simple by nature, but they are hardly boring.

2. Video ads

Video ads are among the most powerful ads on Facebook. They are able to showcase things in action. This is crucial because the power of vision, especially with motion, is much more powerful compared to posts and articles. The video can be powerful even without any audio. However, a video with sound is extremely powerful.

3. Carousel ads

Facebook also provides carousel ads. These are ads that use a series of photos and sometimes videos to market your services or products. Carousel ads are great at highlighting different aspects of a product or even a number of different products. You can also use carousel ads to come up with a big image that sends a powerful yet interesting image.

Other types

Other types of Facebook ads include slideshow ads and collection ads. Slideshow ads are self-explanatory while collection ads are designed specifically for use on mobile devices. Collection ads work together with other applications to enable Facebook users to buy products directly on Facebook without leaving the platform.

Learn how to set up a Facebook ad

1. Begin by setting up goals for your ads

The first step you need to take before placing an ad on Facebook is to determine the reason for the advertisement. You need to have a really good reason for placing Facebook ads. When you set out your goals you will be able to come up with more effective ads. You will also be in a position to measure the effectiveness of your ads because there was a purpose for the ads in the first place.

As an example, let us assume that you desire to have more people download your app onto their phones. In this case, you could have a goal of about 100 downloads per month. This way, when you place an ad, you will be able to measure its effectiveness after the one month period comes to an end. Here are other aims and ambitions that you may have when it comes to Facebook ads.

- Generate new leads
- Boost engagement for our Facebook Page
- Increase the number of attendees to an event
- Boost your Facebook Page engagements
- Increase traffic from Facebook to your website

2. Get to Facebook Ads Manager

Once you have determined the purpose for your Facebook ads, you should then head to Facebook ads manager tool. This is the program that runs and manages all of Facebook's ads. When you visit your Facebook page, check out the "Manage Ads" button and then choose the ads manager from here.

From here, you should navigate to the menu and take a look at the options available to you.

3. Determine your objective with the ad

Once you have your ad ready, you should then indicate what your objective with the ad is. This is important because you are placing the ad hoping to achieve a certain objective. Basically, you will have about 15 different objectives for your campaigns to choose from. These can be categorized into three main ones including conversions, considerations, and creating awareness.

Awareness: When you use Facebook ads to create awareness, then you can hope to achieve some of the following objectives.

- Promote your page
- Boost your posts
- Increase brand awareness
- Reach out to people close to your business
- Extend your reach

If you have a small budget, then you are likely to benefit the most based on the awareness that such ads can create. For instance, at the cost of just $1 each day, you can increase your reach by over 4,000 persons.

Consideration: When it comes to consideration, then some of your objectives are those that actually get your viewers thinking about your establishment and then start learning more about you, the brand, and your products. They include:

- You can redirect followers to a location on Facebook or off
- Increase number of people attending your events
- Have users download and install your app
- Collect business leads
- Have people view your videos

Conversions: As a Facebook user, you may want to buy ads in order to persuade customers to purchase products or pay for services at your store. The store could be online or even a brick and mortar establishment. When it comes to conversions, you could also have the objective of

- Maximize engagement on your app

- Have more engagements on your website
- Promote a catalog or your brand and products
- Have people take up on your offer
- Have customers grace your shop

Once your objective is determined, then you should proceed to name your campaign. Getting more followers on Facebook is desirable for every business and all entrepreneurs. Here are some ways that you can get started on Facebook in order to promote your brand and increase visitor numbers.

4. Determine your budget and audience

You need to determine who your target audience is as far as your business is concerned. This is absolutely crucial if your Facebook ads are to be successful. There are a couple of demographics that determine your audience. These demographics include age, languages, location, gender, behaviors, interests, and connections.

If you can, make sure that you also select advanced settings for better or more accurate targeting. Advanced targeting lets you exclude or include those affiliated with certain apps, pages, or events. You are also able to target people that already bought products or paid for services on your website. This is known as retargeting.

Set your budget

Now that you have determined all the necessary metrics for your ad campaigns, the next step is to determine your budget. You should determine how much money you need to spend on your ads.

Facebook offers you a couple of options. For instance, do you want to pay a daily fee or a lifetime fee? You need to keep in mind that the fee you indicate is the maximum that you are going to pay or intend to pay. If not, then you will get to choose between a lifetime budget and a daily budget. The daily budget is the total amount that you pay each day while a lifetime budget is the maximum amount that you will spend in the lifetime of the ad.

Getting started

Getting started on Facebook is easy. However, you need to be cautious in order to get it right. The first step is to come up with a Facebook marketing plan. This plan will list your objectives and then mention the different ways you will use Facebook to achieve these objectives. Objectives could be to promote your brand, gain more followers, convert leads, retain current customers, and so on.

Once your strategy is in place, you should proceed to open a Facebook business page. Your business profile on this popular social media is really a huge part of your online identity. Therefore, take time to create a professional page that is presentable and with all the relevant contact information. Remember it is from here that you will engage your contacts and followers.

As soon as your page is up and running, you should begin posting content and sharing it with others. There are numerous kinds of content that can be posted on this social media. They include videos, links, posts, memes, photos, stories, and so on. Remember to keep the content fresh, entertaining, and interesting.

Tips and advice on Facebook advertising

As a Facebook account holder and entrepreneur, you should learn a few tips about how to create effective ads targeted at your preferred audience. Here are some tips that you can apply.

1. Experiment with audience targeting

Before investing fully in an ad, first try and target a narrow audience and then see how it goes. If your targeting is accurate, then proceed to broaden it. You can broaden your targeting by adding categories one at a time. You could, for instance, start with a broader category of people within a certain region and then narrow this down more and more until you can accurately get down to an exact niche. This makes it easier for you to be able to understand how to narrow down your target audience and how this affects results.

Using this approach, you will also be able to come up with a variety of ads for different groups depending on your needs on different occasions. For instance, you can have some customers who buy during special occasions and others who are more regular customers. Also, you can come up with ads for first-time customers as compared to ads for existing customers. At other times you may want to have promotions or events targeted at a different audience altogether.

You will need to be careful, though, with the kind of assumptions that you make regarding your audience especially during the selection of your options. For instance, some advertisers use just one language when targeting their customers in Europe even though Europeans in different countries speak different languages.

2. Make use of Facebook pixel

If you want to have more effective ads, then you should make use of Facebook pixel. This is a tool that can support your ads if placed on your website. Pixel will do a couple of things for you including creating lookalike audiences, remarket to audiences that have checked out products or services on your website and also track conversions.

Sometimes you may not be able to make use of all the advanced strategies that you are able to implement using this tool. However, just having this tool on your website is advisable. This way you will also be able to track the performance of your ads and then use any data collected to adjust your marketing message.

3. Make use of the best videos and photos

There are some things that Facebook users just cannot stand. These include unclear images, pixilated or blurry photos, and poor-quality videos. While your words are important and texts are crucial, nothing is more powerful than an image. The visuals that you use need to be top notch, high quality, interesting, informative, and able to impact viewers. If you are selling a product through Facebook, then you should follow Facebook's direction and use photos showing people using your product and how they are benefiting from it. This is more effective than just having an image of the product.

4. Make sure that you test everything

As you use Facebook ads for your business, you should not make any assumptions regarding what to expect. Instead, you should test anything that you are trying out for the first time. Test anything new against something that you tried in the past. This way, you will be able to notice if there were any improvement and benefit based on metrics that you consider important to you.

5. Keep track of performance then optimize

When you place ads on Facebook, it is crucial that you keep a tab on them. When you watch the performance of your ads, you will be able to note what is working and what is not. Any campaign that is generally not performing satisfactorily or as expected, you can withdraw any funds allocated to its budget and reallocate the funds to another fund that is performing as expected.

Basically, if you are placing your first ad on Facebook, then it is advisable to place more than one advert. Since the ads are quite affordable, this will not set you back at all. Placing a number of ads will help you find out which ads are working and which approach is best for your clients. You can only identify a winning campaign after placing a couple of ads and determining the most effective of them all.

Instagram Marketing

Instagram

The social network website Instagram is unlike other social media platforms. Apparently, over 70% of its members live in countries other than the US. Most users also happen to be millennials who range in age from 16 to 24 years. Therefore, if you own a business that targets millennials, then this is the best site for your marketing and advertising campaigns.

There are more females than males on the site, so it is great if you are selling to women. Instagram is also highly recommended for businesses with an international audience. The site is also popular with men even though women are slightly more. Therefore, you can equally target men as much as women. Most users access Instagram from a mobile device so try and optimize your posts and promotional messages towards a mobile platform.

Instagram describes itself as a platform that provides you with an exciting and fun way of sharing your experiences with family and friends through photos, images, and videos.

Instagram is one of the largest social media websites. According to statistics, there are over 5 million businesses that use Instagram to connect with their customers and followers, tell their stories and promote their brands. The website receives a cool 1 billion users each month as of July 2018. This makes Instagram one of the largest and most important social networking websites for both individuals and businesses.

Getting started with Instagram is not at all difficult or challenging. Virtually anyone can open an account and start sharing posts or commenting on content on the website.

Tell your story on Instagram

Instagram is a platform where users share their stories and lifestyles. You do this by sharing mostly photos, images, and videos. Only on rare occasions do users share links or written content. If you live a great life that others envy and admire, you can share pictures of your home, car, office, and your excursions to the store, mall, and so on. Post these on your Instagram page for your follows to see and comment on.

Setting up your Instagram account and profile

The first step that you need to take is to visit the Instagram website or download the app if you are using a handheld device such as a smartphone. You can download the app from Microsoft Store, Google Play Store, or the App Store. Once downloaded, you will clearly see the "Create Profile" button. Click on this button to begin the process of creating your Instagram profile.

Profile photo

You will need to provide a photo to go with your profile. If you are opening a personal account, then you should choose a photo of yourself. However, you can choose a different photo for a business account such as your logo. A logo is great for your business, so you get to advertise or promote your business from the word go.

Once your photo is approved, the next requirement is your profile information. You need to provide both basic as well as detailed information about yourself or your business. You will need to provide basic information such as your names, address, date of birth, email address, and so on. You will also be required to provide a handle or Instagram username. This is the name that will identify you on Instagram. It is unique to you so that there is no confusion.

Post photos and videos

As soon as you provide the basic information required, you will need to verify your account via your email address. Posting is really easy. All you will need to do is to click on the posting icon and then select the video or photo you would like to post. Remember to select high quality, memorable, impressive, colorful images, and videos that will tell your story or showcase your brand.

Why Choose Instagram Marketing

Instagram is probably the social network that provides the most ideal platform for businesses. When it works, then it works really well. While the success rates will generally vary across the board, most businesses experience a much better return compared to most other social media platforms.

To be successful on Instagram as an entrepreneur, then your product should be tangible with visual properties such as colorful and presentable. This way, you can take professional shots of the product from different angles and then share them with your followers and also post them in your campaign ads.

Your product should also be geared towards young consumers, millennials, men and women, as well and international customers. If your product provides this, then you are on your way to success with Instagram marketing.

Instagram marketing information

The average engagement for ads and posts stands at 3.3% for major brands compared to only 0.07% on Twitter. Also, Instagram users are 25% more likely to be successful and wealthy which means they increase your chances of success. Also, almost over 20% of all web users have an Instagram account.

Success with Instagram marketing

Instagram is totally different from all other social media websites. Therefore, if you were successful on other social networks like

Facebook, you will want to look at Instagram afresh. Even then, while it is slightly different from other social networks, the basics of getting your campaigns still apply.

The first thing you'll have to do is to take a closer look at what your target audience are responding to. What kind of topics, images, and videos do they seem to like and share? Also, check out what other brands are posting. Are they sharing funny videos or serious marketing messages? Learn what works for them and what does not. From here you will learn a lot about Instagram marketing and what approach is best.

Tips for success with Instagram marketing

Outsource the marketing aspect: Social media marketing can be quite time consuming and involving. If you are very busy with your business or other engagements elsewhere, then you should consider outsourcing the marketing process to a third party. There are plenty of digital marketers and marketing firms out there that can handle the process for you. You can still get involved in the marketing strategy and ad campaign creation. You can also monitor the progress, performance, and outcome of your campaigns.

Consider the financial resources needed: You will need to consider the financial aspect of posting ads on Instagram. When it comes to budgeting for the marketing campaign, you should consider the cost of hiring an ad firm as well as how long you want your campaign to run and so on.

Time is also a factor: Social media marketing takes time before the benefits or effects are noticeable. Therefore, do not spend all your time coming up with marketing strategies and things of that nature. If you are more focused on the intricacies of your business, then hire someone to help with this aspect. You may also outsource the function to someone else as has already been discussed.

Creativity: As a brand marketing on such a powerful and crucial platform, you need to ensure that you are as creative as possible.

This means coming up with top-notch, impactful, memorable, and catchy ads that will impact viewers and compel them to act like you want them to. With a great strategy and suitable software, especially video editing software, you can prepare high-quality videos that your audience and the general public will appreciate.

Benefits of Instagram marketing

1. Brand awareness: One of the benefits of Instagram marketing is that it helps promote your brand to millions of users. Keep in mind that over 20% of all internet users have an Instagram account, so the chances of your message being seen are very high.

2. Customer feedback: When you place ads and other forms of marketing campaigns on Instagram, you receive customer feedback. Customer feedback is crucial for brands and businesses. You get to learn first-hand what your customers think about your products and services. The benefit, in this case, is that you get to receive customer feedback almost instantly.

3. Relationship building: If you wish to build relationships with customers, followers, and others, then Instagram is the best platform for you. Here you can allow your brand to express its amazing properties and benefits to your viewers. Use photos, images, memes, and videos to express personality and reach out to even more consumers.

4. Increase your interests and sales: When your brand grows then sales will follow almost automatically. Customers basically love good quality products so if your brand displays quality and provides a service or addresses a need that consumers have, then they will definitely purchase from you.

5. Potential to attract a new demographic: Since Instagram is a public platform, your brand and products can be viewed by numerous users especially if you have a public page. If you wish to attract an additional demographic such as international buyers, then Instagram provides you with an excellent opportunity to achieve this.

Tips on uploading the best Instagram photo

Most of the photos that you will upload to your Instagram will either be domiciled on your device or online. When you choose a photo to upload on Instagram, it can be oriented as either a landscape or portrait position. Select a photo that you want and then make any adjustments you wish such as adjust color, switch orientation, zoom, add captions, and so on. When you feel the image looks just right, you may then post it.

Instagram allows you to upload a maximum of 10 images and videos at one go. Therefore, if you wish to upload multiple images, Instagram provides you with the opportunity to do so. There is an icon consisting of two envelopes. Simply click this icon in order to upload multiple images.

You can also upload images and then schedule the posting. This is an excellent feature because posting times are crucial. If you are busy with little time to spend on your Instagram account, simply use the scheduling posting tool provided. This way, you will have your images posted at the times and dates that you choose. If you think most of your viewers or customers log onto Instagram in the evenings, then schedule your photos to be posted in the evening for maximum effect.

Additional Instagram tips

1. Focus on custom audiences and preferred demographics: Instagram allows you to send your marketing messages to a select group of individuals. You can choose who receives your messages in order to improve effectiveness. The select audience could include customers you have interacted with in the past, individuals on your email list, or even an audience that you created based on preferred criteria.

2. Make irresistible offers: Instagram is a very visual platform, and users often spend time viewing different posts including images and videos. With the right kind of content and message, you can take advantage of the platform and attract customers to your platform.

3. Make use of lookalike audience: One advantage that Instagram has is that it can help you identify a similar audience to the one that you seek. Therefore, after marketing to your current audience, you can then find a very similar audience to market to. This is a very effective approach that will help increase your reach.

4. Make use of hashtags: One of the most powerful features on Instagram is the hashtag. This platform is really driven by hashtags so while others may not take them seriously, you really should. They have a powerful way of connecting niche audiences and sharing a message.

5. Make use of custom images: While Instagram is huge on photos and images, stock photos are not allowed so make use of custom images of real people.

Editing your photos

Photos also need to be edited in some instances. There are various tools provided for editing photos. Here are some of the things that you can do with your posts.

Write a caption: when you post media such as videos and photos, you should add a caption. A caption is almost like a title. It headlines the image and provides a brief description so that others can learn more about the images and understand what message you are putting out for your viewers.

You can add tags or tag users that you believe need to view your post. You can also tag influential people, social media influencers, and anyone else that you like. Users often have what is known as handle or username. Make use of these handles so that more people get to view your posts. Also, use hashtags whenever possible. A hashtag often refers to a topic that is popular and being discussed.

Whenever people discuss a particular topic via a hashtag, then your image will appear through these conversations which help to increase your reach.

Add a location: Anytime that you post items on your social media, you should take the time to add your location. This can be very helpful because it means your posts will appear whenever anyone mentions your location.

Share posts across social media: It is now easier than ever to share your content with others on social media. You can share your content including images and videos not just with followers on Instagram but with others on other social networks such as Facebook and Twitter. This greatly increases your reach and provides more opportunities for your brand and products.

Chapter 6: Marketing and Selling Online

YouTube Marketing

Did you know that YouTube is one of the largest and most popular search engines in the world? Yes, YouTube is second only to Google which is the world's largest search engine. Millions of users log in to YouTube each day to search for information, news, funny stories, entertaining content, and so much more.

Businesses, both big and small, have increasingly been using YouTube for their marketing purposes. Since numerous users are on this social networking site, it makes sense to post ads and marketing campaigns on the platform. Chances are that your potential customers are on the platform as well. If you can place targeted messages aimed at a certain demographic, then you will increase your chances of increasing your reach, gaining more followers, creating brand awareness, and acquiring new customers.

YouTube is the second most popular website

According to Alexa.com, a platform that ranks websites based on visitor numbers, YouTube is the world's second most popular website. While most people don't think of it as a search engine, more searches are conducted here than most other search engines. It enjoys visits from more than a billion active users and is available in over 76 different languages. Also, 33% of the time people spend online is used to watch videos.

Over 59% of business and company executives prefer to spend their time watching videos rather than read pages and pages of text. Also, more people in the age range between 18 – 49 access YouTube than any mobile, cable, or broadcast network. Over 3.25 billion hours of videos are watched each month on YouTube. All this information shows that chances are very high that your customers, both current and future, are on YouTube.

YouTube is an excellent marketing platform. It allows users to create content and present it on the platform for viewers to enjoy and share. As a business owner and marketer, you can capitalize on YouTube to improve your brand presence and SEO ranking. As a business owner and entrepreneur, it is crucial to learn how to create great marketing content and videos then posting these on YouTube.

Create a YouTube channel

The first step in marketing on YouTube is to create a YouTube channel. However, maintaining a highly effective and good quality channel is not easy. It takes a lot of time to build up one because high-quality videos are costly to produce. On all social media sites, people post all other kinds of content. However, on YouTube, you can only post video content. Channels are created for uploading and hosting lots of content, so if you plan to upload just one video, then there is no need to create a channel.

Creating YouTube videos requires that you take to plan, strategize, make considerations, create videos, edit, and then market and analyze the performance. You should come up with plans and goals for your content and then use available tools to analyze the performance. The reason why you need to analyze how your videos perform is to understand what your viewers and customers think, what they are saying, and the tactics that are effective.

1. Create an account

Your first step even before grabbing your video camera is to create an account. This is not very simple because YouTube is owned by Google and as such you will need a Google account. As such, if you have a Gmail account, then you can easily start your own YouTube account and all other Google-affiliated accounts. It would, therefore, be easier to open your own Gmail account.

Once your Gmail account is verified and operation, you should then set up a YouTube brand account. At this stage, you are ready to upload content onto your YouTube account. However, before doing that, you should brand your account. Remember that you want to take advantage of the huge audience and massive viewership on YouTube. You will use your brand account to gain access to create an immense experience as well as editing permissions.

2. Sign in to YouTube

First, go to YouTube's homepage. This is at the URL www.youtube.com. Once on this page, you should confirm that you are logged in. Simply check at the top left-hand side corner of your YouTube page. If you are not logged, then you can do so from the same top-left corner. As soon as you log in, you will see a couple of buttons including "My Channel." Click on this button and create your channel. You can use your personal or business name.

It is advisable to use your brand name here because you really should be promoting your brand. Please note that you can always change your channel name should the need to do so arise. Therefore, do not worry too much about it as you can make changes from the settings page later.

3. Customize your channel

Now that you have your YouTube channel up and running, you should now customize it. Customization will help you to personalize it so that your followers, viewers and everyone else can recognize your channel and tell apart from all others. For starters, you will need to add an icon and some channel artwork. Anyone visiting your channel will see these first. Make them consistent and easy to remember. This way, any confusion with other channels will be eliminated, and your faithful customers, followers, and viewers will be able to identify you and find you easily. You channel icon is very similar to a profile photo on other social media. If you can keep this consistent, then you will fare really well in your social media marketing strategy.

Once these are set up, you should then provide your business details including address, company email, and channel description. You should also include direct links to your company website so any interested person can visit your website directly should they need to. You should also try and provide additional information about the content you are posting. For instance, are you posting videos about a particular topic or a variety of topics?

When creating videos for your channel, try and focus on showing your audience what the video is all about. Also, remember to request them to subscribe to your channel for more and better videos. A trailer that you prepare to whet your visitor's appetite will not be smothered by ads. This allows your audience to focus on your content before watching the entire video.

When you receive more than 100 subscribers, then your channel will become eligible for URL customization. However, to qualify, you will also need to have a channel art and an icon, and your channel should be at least 30 days old. Remember that you can assign other members of your team access to the account by adding their Gmail accounts. This way, they will be able to log onto the channel through their accounts and implement your marketing strategies or post videos.

Ideally, you can grant access to your channel at three different levels. These are the owner, manager, and communications manager. If you are the owner, you get to enjoy full editing rights over all your Google assets. You can remove or add managers as well as respond to comments, and alter business information. All the others have lesser roles in comparison and can be removed from the account at any time.

SEO optimization for your YouTube videos

Remember that YouTube is also a search engine. As such, you will need to optimize your videos in order to get them to rank on the first page of search results.

Creating high-quality videos for your channel is just half the work done. You will still need to optimize your videos. There are things that you can do so that your videos rank highly on both YouTube and Google.

Metadata

One of the most crucial steps in optimizing your videos is to focus on the Metadata. You need to create and optimize the metadata using appropriate keywords. Basically, metadata refers to information about your video that you put out there for your viewers. This information briefly lets users or viewers learn what the video is all about.

It includes video category, title, subtitles, tags, description, thumbnails and closed captions. When you create your metadata and provide the correct information, then YouTube will index it correctly and ensure that it appears in searches when people search for similar videos.

Title

Another important SEO aspect is optimization of your title. You need to optimize the description and title of your YouTube videos. People will always read the title of your YouTube video first. Therefore, ensure that it is compelling and clear. A good title is one that is catchy and will cause users to pause during a search and click on your video. Consider doing some keyword research for your videos. Also, ensure that your keywords are not longer than 60 characters, so they are not cut off in results pages.

Description

As you write your video description, you should focus on the first three lines because that is what YouTube will display after a search is conducted. If viewers want to read more than the first three lines, then they will need to click on the "Show More" tab. Therefore, include all important links as well as keywords at the initial stages of your description. Make sure you use essential or main keywords in order to optimize this aspect of your YouTube video.

You will also need to optimize your tags, category, and thumbnails in the same manner. If you follow these optimization tips and techniques, then you can trust that your video will rank highly on any YouTube search results based on your specific keywords.

YouTube videos

Once your videos are posted and you start receiving viewers, you should ensure that you remain honest and straightforward with your followers. As a business and even for individuals, providing credible information is crucial. This will ensure that you gain trust from your viewers. When you establish trust, then your followers will easily be converted to loyal paying customers.

After posting a video, your followers and other viewers are likely to comment on it. When they do, you should engage them rather than ignore them. Engaging your followers will ensure that they keep coming back and can be converted to leads.

Do not forget to link back your videos to your website. This way, if your customers love your content, trust you, and wish to know more about you, then you should make it easy for them to find your website. A simple link is in most cases sufficient.

Building Trust

Without regular interactions between brands and customers, some organizations would encounter immense marketing challenges. Platforms such as YouTube provide excellent opportunities for brands to engage with their customers and prospects. Such relationships help to build trust, and a community will form around your brand.

Make sure to publish honest content

As a business owner, you need to ensure that everything that you do is forthright and honest. Your followers, as well as the general public, will trust you when you are honest and forthright. This also means that you should publish honest content at all times. This is content that comes from the heart. It does appeal to followers so make use of it.

Engage with your followers

Another crucial advice that you need to always apply is to engage your customers and followers directly. Social media is always a two-way street, so you need to ensure that you give as much as you take. You should, for instance, respond to comments, ask follow up questions and also like and leave comments on your followers' posts.

Put yourself out as an authority

YouTube users are very likely to follow you and trust you if they believe you are an authority in your niche. You become an authority when you provide excellent content about a niche continuously for a period of time. If you can answer your viewers' questions and address different topics, you will sooner or later be considered an authority in the field.

Focus on providing useful content

You also need to provide content that is helpful to your community of followers and viewers. A lot of people get onto social media seeking help, guidance, and advice. It is content producers like you that they look up to for assistance. If you can provide helpful content time and time again, then you will be able to gain the trust of your followers.

Increase traffic to your YouTube channel

It is impressive to note that over 500 million hours of YouTube videos are watched each day. The sad part is that less than 15% of business owners leverage on this viewership to promote their businesses. Fortunately, there are ways available to you to increase traffic to your YouTube channel.

Produce high-quality content

There is nothing that can increase your reach and attract viewers to your YouTube channel that killer content. If you want to engage an audience for hours and retain them for a long time, ensure that you routinely develop and deliver high value, informative, and entertaining content.

Optimize your YouTube videos

Even YouTube content needs to be optimized. Remember that YouTube is the world's second largest search engine. If you are able to competently optimize your content, then you can expect to attract more YouTube traffic to your website.

Use tools provided by YouTube to increase traffic

YouTube provides plenty of tools which you can use in order to optimize your content. For instance, you can use video editing software to help produce quality content. There is also a tool known as Tube Buddy which is designed to help with the management of smaller tasks. These tools will definitely boost your traffic.

Social Media Tips and Advice

Now that you have a presence in more social media websites, you need to have a proper approach in order to capitalize on the numerous marketing opportunities available. There is some etiquette that you will need to observe to increase your reach, attract more followers, promote your brands, attract more customers, and increase profits.

Engage with others

The first rule of thumb is that you should engage with followers and viewers. If you post content such as photos, videos, links to blogs, images and so on, then respond to all who leave comments. If a viewer asks questions, try, and answer the questions. If another leaves a positive comment, thank them and invite them to become a follower or subscriber.

Also, respond to anyone who shares or posts content. If your followers share content with them, make sure that you engage them in the most suitable manner. If they share content, then comment on the content and if they share a video then watch it and leave a positive comment. Some posts can be shared, and others liked. Engaging involves lots of different activity. The important thing is to be in regular communication with your followers. This will not only create a bond but will also enhance trust and draw them closer to you.

Give free value

Another crucial step that you need to keep in mind is to provide lots and lots of free value. This is crucial if you are to build trust. Find out what people within your industry are interested in or what problems bother them the most. When you can establish their problems and challenges, provide useful and practical solutions. Write blogs, provide images, research solutions, and get the best answers on each topic. Leave comments on blogs, websites, and different social media. When you do so, share a link to your blog where the solution can be found.

Keep doing this for a long time until people within your industry begin trusting you. You will need to do this for a period of six to nine months until trust is completely established and your authority on a subject matter is established. As you provide value and solutions, they will not only trust you but will view you as an industry leader, a guru, and expert in your field. It is only after you establish yourself that they will begin taking your advice and eventually start buying products or services from you.

How to provide free value

There are different ways of providing free value to viewers, followers, and social media users. You could provide free e-books full of relevant information within a certain niche. When you produce an e-book, make sure it is of very high quality. The content needs to be well written, claims should be backed up by facts, solutions to people's problems should be clearly defined, and any necessary media such as images, graphs, or links provided as well.

Remember to ask for email addresses when you provide the free e-books. Building an e-mail list of people within your niche is an excellent marketing strategy which you can later use when applying email marketing strategy.

Also, share blogs that you have written. Blogs provide an excellent platform for providing value and information. Share links to your blogs on social media and let others visit your blogs and read your content. Make sure you invite the readers to leave comments on your blogs and engage with them when they do. Also, collect emails of followers who come to your blog and engage with them. Just don't start pushing anything just yet until the time is right.

You can also provide stories and share real-life experiences. Users often love people who are real and who they can relate to. They normally dislike corporate types who are cold and are often too busy for their customers. So provide value most of the time but also share stories, posts, and all things that will add value to your readers.

Examples

You could begin your posts in a casual manner and say things such as, "Hey guys, here are 5 ways of solving that problem." Or you can perhaps say, "Here is something I tried that really worked." Then, share a link to the solution. Alternatively, you can invite all followers on one social media site to follow you on another site. Most people on Instagram also have a Facebook page so invite them from one platform to follow you on another platform and then follow them back.

Email Marketing

There are numerous marketing methods that you can use when you are an online entrepreneur. One of these is email marketing. For a while, you have been collecting e-mail when you shared value with your readers, followers, and general internet users.

There are various tools available to enable you to collect emails effectively and accurately. Once you have these emails, you should build a list. An email list provides you with an easy and effective way of contacting your readers. Remember that these readers are individuals within your industry who are interested in your posts and have gained value from your knowledge.

One of the best things that you can do with your online popularity is to collect as many email address from your viewers. You can then begin sending them emails telling them about important products that you have or any upcoming events. Let us say you have a business product launch or similar event, you should create high-quality emails and invite all your followers to the event.

Even as you send out these emails, try and offer an incentive. These incentives may include freebies, discounts, vouchers, and offers. Most consumers love discounted offers so do this to entice probably the first one hundred customers for instance. Email marketing is a very effective marketing strategy which can bring you success such as increased reach, engagements, more customers and increased profits.

Begin selling your products or providing services

Now that you have been giving for so long and providing a lot of value, it is time to begin taking. You do this by selling your products to your customers. At this stage, you should start advertising your products and brand and invite customers to your social media sites or websites where they can buy your products. If you applied your marketing strategy appropriately, then you should expect high sales with serious engagements across social media platforms and your website.

You can sell directly through your website or as an affiliate. There are numerous companies with high-quality products that offer affiliate products. Think about places such as Amazon Associates and Click Bank. These are established firms with successful affiliate marketing programs that are quite popular.

Affiliate marketing simply means selling on behalf of someone else. For instance, you can sell products within your industry but available on sites such as Amazon. If you provide high-quality information and present yourself as an expert, then your readers will trust you as an expert and will definitely buy products from you.

Remember that if you want to Affiliate Products, make sure you have tried the product itself and are 100% guaranteed that your audience are going to be happy with the product or service.

Best Places To Find Affiliate Products?

You can find affiliate products and services through websites such as:

- ClickBank
- Amazon Associates
- And emailing or messaging the business or business owner directly

Teach Others

By this stage, if you want, you are sufficiently experienced to teach, coach, mentor and train others. This is because you have pretty much acquired experience across all the stages of entrepreneurship. Teach interested persons about finding a niche, how to become an entrepreneur, how to start an online store, how to promote their brands and products, marketing across social media, optimization for search engines, and so much more.

You can teach by selling e-books or courses. There are sites that offer affiliate courses at a 50% commission. Teach whatever pleases you or has the greatest demand. At this stage, you can declare yourself an authority and expert in your niche so consumers and upcoming entrepreneurs will follow you and listen to your advice.

Conclusion

By now, you have learned a lot about how to become an entrepreneur and an expert in your industry. You have also learned how to become a successful marketer, an entrepreneur, and how to use social media sites for advertising and marketing purposes.

Building a brand may take time, but you will eventually get there. Do not take any shortcuts or disregard the information provided by experts. Remember that the internet is a global platform with billions of users. Therefore, if you build a strong brand and apply a great marketing strategy, then you can become as successful as you want and become a millionaire!

Finally if you found this book helpful, please leave a review on Amazon as it allows me to keep producing quality books.

www.ingramcontent.com/pod-product-compliance
Lightning Source LLC
Chambersburg PA
CBHW071231210326
41597CB00016B/2006